SONGS FOR A TIME YET TO COME

For here we do not have an enduring city, but we are looking for the city that is to come.

Hebrews 13:14

SONGS FOR A TIME YET TO COME

Dave Jackson

CONTENTS

Preface   ix

Part 1: The Redeeming God

Songs of Celebration   3

Songs of Heaven   13

Songs of Perspective   21

Songs of Redemption   31

Songs of Salvation   41

Songs of Servanthood   51

Songs of Submission   61

Songs of Transformation   71

Songs of Truth   81

Part 2: The Eternal God

Songs of Contemplation   91

Songs of Creation   99

Songs of Enlightenment   111

Songs of Eternity   123

Songs of Hope   129

Songs of Invitation   141

Songs of Purpose   151

Songs of the Kingdom Come   161

Songs of Worth   169

Part 3: The Compassionate God

Songs of Comfort   179

Songs of Commitment   189

Songs of Compassion   197

Songs of Doubt   205

Songs of Freedom   213

Songs of Integrity   223

Songs of Perseverance   233

Songs of the Lost   243

Part 4: The Merciful God

Songs of Contrition   255

Songs of Faith   267

Songs of Forgiveness   277

Songs of Grace   285

Songs of Humility   295

Songs of Mercy   303

Songs of Sacrifice   313

Songs of Thanksgiving   323

Part 5: The Loving God

Songs of Community   333

Songs of Connection   341

Songs of Insight   347

Songs of Loving   355

Songs of Passion   365

Songs of Prayer   373

Songs of Sharing   383

Songs of the Spirit   393

Songs of Wisdom   401

PREFACE

A long time in the making

This book has been taking shape for a very long time, with the collection of poems spanning more than forty-five years of writing. The oldest was penned as long ago as 1978, when I was still in my teens; others are from various times in the intervening years; and with many more written more recently, particularly in the period 2020-2024.

The basic concept and initial ideas for the book were first conceived many years ago; but it has only been in recent times that retirement from the workplace has led both to a significant increase in the writing of new material and the time and opportunity to pull everything together into this one volume.

While the poems are principally on Christian themes, my sense is that many of the topics covered are of more general application and may also resonate with a wider readership in today's World.

My hope is that whatever life journey people are on, they may in differing ways and in different measures be able to draw encouragement, comfort, and inspiration from the reflections and from the accompanying poems.

In all of this, my purpose has been for each reflection to offer some initial thoughts, with the poems exploring the subject further from various perspectives, and the photographs adding colour. The latter, like the poems, span a period of many years.

The reflections and the poems express my personal understanding of Scripture and of the Christian faith. My readers may, of course, have different views; it is up to them to draw their own conclusions on the matters covered.

Why poetry?

Although it seems to be less popular and not as widely read as other forms of literature, the brevity and compactness of a poem have the power to connect to our minds and imaginations in unique and special ways.

Through the use of example, metaphor, imagery, and by the often-unusual juxtaposition of otherwise familiar words and phrases, a poem can engage the reader's thoughts and emotions at a level where more straightforward writing may be unable to do so.

Poems can make us smile; they may make us cry ('but in a good way', as a friend once observed!); and they can move us deeply, by finding pertinent words to express particular feelings and experiences.

There is also something special about poetry that can lead two people, reading the same poem, to find that the words speak to them individually in very different (and sometimes quite personal) ways.

Thanks

No introduction would be complete without a mention of those who have encouraged me in my writing over the years and who have motivated me to bring this collection together at last.

I am grateful to those of my Church leaders, both past and present, who have each in their own way variously informed and inspired, encouraged and enlightened me: you know who you are!

I have also been greatly supported and nurtured over many years by immediate family, by close friends, and by my Christian brothers and sisters in the Church families to which I have been privileged to belong.

I am especially grateful to both my daughter Charlotte and my son Rory, who read through my initial draft and who made a number of insightful comments and helpful suggestions for improvement!

But, above all others, my mainstay through everything has been Helen, my beautiful, brilliant, wife, to whom this book is dedicated, with love.

Dave Jackson
Easter 2024

SONGS FOR A TIME YET TO COME

PART 1: THE REDEEMING GOD

SONGS OF CELEBRATION

When [the Magi] saw the star, they were overjoyed. On coming to the house, they saw the child with his mother Mary, and they bowed down and worshipped him.

Matthew 2:10-11

Christmas is coming...

Christmas: a time for giving and receiving. Particularly in our secular, post-modern Western World, Christmas has become more than ever a time of year reflecting the pervasive materialism that impairs all our lives. There seems to be a never-ending obsession with 'things': a need to own the fastest car, the most hi-tech gadget, the latest fashion, and so on.

Almost lost amongst this rampant commercialism are the muffled sounds of what Christmas is really about – a celebration of the birth of the most important person who has ever lived: Jesus Christ, the Son of God. This is the true Christmas gift – lasting, eternal and priceless.

For many, Christmas can be a time of great excitement ('just what is in that package that arrived in the post today?'), but it can also be tinged with anxiety ('how am I going to pay for all of this?'). While there is nothing inherently wrong in spending hard-earned cash on items that bring comfort and pleasure, those benefits are transient and ultimately an illusion. Their shine soon fades and it is all too easy quickly to succumb to a renewed craving for the 'next big thing' on the market.

Are we really prepared to settle for what will only too soon become last year's model? And are we just chasing after rainbows?

What is it that brings us true satisfaction in life? We soon discover that our relentless pursuit of all that the World has to offer will not, after all, deliver the contentment that we seek.

Should we not, perhaps, be seeking instead to take hold of the ultimate – and permanent – gift of eternal fulfilment, that is so generously and freely offered to all of us, ours for the taking if we choose to accept it?

The Present

It's Christmas again – are we ready and waiting?
Is everything done, are we anticipating
The turkey, the tinsel, the lights on the tree,
Will our Christmas be all that we hope it will be?

But are we so swamped by the things to be done
That we've lost any focus, before it's begun:
Forgetting our purpose, and losing all reason,
Immersed by the frantic demands of the season.

With tasks to complete, we have hardly stopped racing
From pillar to post, with the deadline we're facing;
Wrapped up in a process we have to get right,
So that everything's done by the twenty-fourth night.

We set so much stock by the gifts we supply,
But the reason for giving them passes us by.
Are we truly content with the baubles we're sold?
Perhaps all that glitters is not really gold.

The joy from the gaudy assortment we buy
Lasts only for moments, however we try;
Our retailing frenzy holds little in store,
When we sense in our hearts that there has to be more.

No sumptuous feasting on seasonal fare
Can give us a foretaste of all we can share,
If we take a short breath, if we stop in our tracks,
To expose what this aimless activity lacks.

The image familiar, the clichés abound,
That blind us from seeing a gift so profound:
Those two wooden branches that make up the Cross
Where God gave, and forgave, and redeemed all our loss.

No sparkling displays, or the Christmas tree lights,
Can reach even close to the glorious heights
That God bids us to seek at the foot of the tree:
He offers us life, everlasting, for free.

Christmas Eve

Where will our true focus be, this Christmas Eve?
What deep in our hearts do we really believe?
Are we so swept up in the seasonal mood
That it's all about presents and far too much food,
Minds set on receiving, instead of the giving
Of One sacrificing His all for our living?

Our gaze so transfixed on the baubles and beads,
We are losing all sight, what the World surely needs,
With all we've stored up to indulge every craving:
We're ignoring the One with the greatest of saving.

If despite the great love that our Saviour has shown,
We still turn our thoughts inwards, look out for our own,
For the comforts we think only money can buy:
We'll be blind to the star burning bright in the sky.

Stuck on repeat, as the years keep on turning,
The World's empty gifts cannot meet our true yearning,
Or awaken our souls that too long have been sleeping:
For it's only in God that we'll find what's worth keeping.

If we look to the heavens and choose to believe,
Then our hearts may discover a new Christmas Eve,
A joy we can only by God's grace afford:
Our baubles exchanged for the gift of the Lord.

Still Shining

The star comes to rest on the lowliest stable,
The story no myth or some fanciful fable,
But something so real it's as if we can feel it
So deep in our souls, even time cannot steal it.

The promise of life gives us every reason
To hold on to this joy, and not just for the season;
Yet too soon it becomes one more story we're hearing,
Lost in the noise of the new year appearing.

Too often we watch from a distant location,
The cares of our lives soon replacing elation
At the grace of our God who stepped down to receive us,
Who will one day return, who is never to leave us.

If we're letting our wonder of the child in the manger
Fade so soon from the memory, we make Him a stranger;
Yet He still longs to meet us, to pour out His glory,
Every page of our lives in a wondrous story.

Our Lord came to Earth as the greatest life giver,
Let's embrace all the fullness He came to deliver,
And not place our trust on the World's empty altars;
For the star is still shining: its light never falters.

The Next Day

What did the Magi think the next day,
As they mounted their camels and went on their way?
Did they look at the stars with a different eye,
What new signs did they see in the faraway sky?
If they sensed who it was they were coming to bless,
Did they prize their own wisdom a little bit less?

What did the Earthly king think the next day
When he heard that the Magi had gone their own way?
Did he fear something different had happened, so strange,
Yet his heart remained closed and unable to change?

What did the innkeeper think the next day
Once the child and His parents had gone on their way?
Would he hope to have more than a low stable stall
So when travellers arrived, there'd be room for them all?

What did the shepherds think the next day,
When their flocks had been gathered, with none left astray?
Did they wonder in awe at the Heavenly choir
That was praising the Lamb, ever lifting Him higher?

And just what did Joseph think the next day?
Did he marvel how God had directed the way,
That by faith in the Lord and by trust in his bride,
They had been kept secure, as he stayed by her side?

And, indeed, what did Mary think the next day
As she cradled her child in the warmth of the hay?
Did she know that God's Kingdom had landed on Earth,
And that everything changed from the time of His birth?

So, what will we think when we greet the next day,
When the gifts that we cherish are all put away?
Will we stand in the light or be left in the shade,
Will the star still be shining, or will it just fade?

What will we think and how should we pray,
As we look for His leading a different way?
If all our tomorrows will be the next day
Will we welcome Him in; will we ask Him to stay?

Gathering In

In a place far away, at a time long ago,
Rose a star in the east with a Heavenly glow;
And a choir of angels could not help but sing:
Announcing the coming of Jesus the King.

And out of the dark, shepherds hearing the call,
Followed the star to a low stable stall,
Where with others they worshipped their newly born Lord,
On whom all the favour of God had been poured.

With so many today who still flock to His side,
Still the praises continue with arms open wide;
Let's embrace all the wonder from when He first came,
Give the glory that's due to His glorious name.

For, two thousand years on, with a watch still to keep,
He is gathering in, gently tending His sheep,
As the songs of the angels give unending praise
To the Lord everlasting, the Ancient of Days!

SONGS OF HEAVEN

---

*But in keeping with his promise we are looking forward to a
new heaven and a new earth, the home of righteousness.*

2 Peter 3:13

On Cloud Nine?

What will Heaven really be like? The truth is that much of the detail remains hidden from us; our limited minds and imaginations are incapable of taking on board more than a fraction of the extraordinary things that await us, when we are raised to life with Jesus.

But even in our highly secular modern society, the concept of 'Heaven' still takes centre stage in so much of our language, our thinking, and our behaviour. How often have we heard the following sort of comments made, in our everyday lives:

'...it must have been Heaven-sent...': suggesting the unexpected provision of something miraculous;

'...it's Heavenly...': experiencing something of great pleasure;

'...they are in Heaven now...': taking comfort, in grief, that lost loved ones are now in an eternally safe place;

'...it's like Heaven on Earth...': speaking of the most wonderful place imaginable and the thought that there could be nothing better;

'...Heaven only knows...': implying that there is perhaps a place of knowledge and understanding that is beyond our human reach.

All well and good. But none of these, in themselves, describe the Heaven that followers of Jesus are looking forward to.

Heaven, in its true sense, is about our being permanently in the eternal presence of God, enjoying the privilege of an intimate relationship of love and trust with him. It is a complete transformation from the pale mortal existence that we presently experience.

One way of trying to get our heads around the enormity of this might be to think of a time, a place, an experience in our life that was the most joyous, the most satisfying, the most fulfilling; where we were lost in the moment, free from all our cares and concerns. Then, multiply that several billion times, and realise that even then this would barely scratch the surface of what it will be like to live in perfect harmony with God, forever, in Heaven.

The World we know will not be entirely swept away and replaced by something different. Rather, it will be renewed and restored to the way that it was always intended to be, since the beginning of time. A World that was once damaged and degraded by sin will instead be transformed into a World in perfect harmony with God.

The small glimpses of Heaven that we can experience now will be as nothing to what awaits us when all is made new.

And we too will be individually restored. We can be sure that this is so, from the experience of Jesus' last days on Earth following his resurrection.

He still inhabited a body that outwardly was recognisably the same as before his death. Ultimately, those to whom he appeared were left in no doubt as to who this was. He was not some ethereal being; he was a real, flesh and blood person. They could see and touch the still visible wounds in his hands and side; and he shared a meal and ate food with them.

And yet, he was fundamentally different from before. The resurrected body that he inhabited had been radically changed, to one that was free from mortal limitations and which was fully restored and equipped for an eternal existence with God in Heaven.

In the same way, while the resurrected bodies that we inhabit may, perhaps, in some way still be physically recognisable as before, qualitatively they will be entirely different. No longer subject to decay and death, 'the perishable has been clothed with the imperishable' (1 Corinthians 15:54); we too will have bodies made ready for Heaven, that will last through all eternity.

'Well, when you put it like that…!'

Set Alight

It feels as if the World will not stop burning,
That calmer times will never be returning;
It makes me wonder where all this is heading,
When desolation is forever spreading.

It seems each day that everything is flaming,
But there's nobody else we should be blaming,
For we have stripped the planet of its cover,
And shown ourselves to be no nature-lover.

We face an ever-growing conflagration,
That's overwhelming each and every nation,
The World descending to its closing hour,
With nothing left, no single leafy bower;
Our blood runs cold, yet still there's overheating
That's far beyond our power to be defeating.

I long to see the World alight and blazing:
Not burning trees, but something so amazing;
I'm searching for a different kind of fire,
Not one that will become our funeral pyre.
For every faithful soul our Lord will cherish,
And, by His grace, He will not let us perish.
This song may end, but we will still be singing,
To praise Him for His grace and mercy bringing,
With all that's passed swept up in transformation:
Out of the ashes, God brings restoration.

Awaken

How I wish to close my eyes, to wake where God is waiting
To lead me to a place that I'm by faith anticipating;
To leave behind this tangled web that threatens to enfold me;
Instead, embrace the Word of God and all that He has told me.

How I want to lay my head forever on His shoulder,
To see the flame burst into life and not just left to smoulder;
To find a courage not my own, but of my Saviour's making,
To follow as He calls me, come, all other ways forsaking.

How I hope, with open eyes, to follow where He's leading,
To let Him have the final say: His grace in me succeeding.
But until then I know that I can never be forsaken,
Assured the day is coming when in Heaven I awaken.

How I long to sleep the sleep that wakens me forever,
That brings me to a place that can't be earned by my endeavour;
Protected from the burning Sun, His hand to shield and shade me,
Accepting this great gift of love from God, the One who made me.

Everlasting

It's said that time runs quicker as we move towards the close,
To bring us to a final day that only Heaven knows;
The hand is moving forward and can never be reversed;
What we thought was first is last and last is coming first.

Time that once moved slowly is now running ever fast,
The future overtaking every distant memory passed;
But age brings new perspective as the change comes into view,
We see that this was just a pause, that we're now passing through.

Days that stretched before us all too swiftly pass us by;
Gone, before we notice, in the blinking of an eye.
Yet, just around the corner, an eternity awaiting,
With every saint in Heaven our arrival celebrating.

For this is not an ending that is calling for escape;
But, reaching for the finish line, we're glad to break the tape.
And when the clock is stopping, we'll be ready to depart:
To welcome that the last is first, a glorious new start!

Days Are Coming

The days are coming, says the Lord,
We'll be adorned in robes of white,
When all God's goodness will be poured,
And we will see Him, shining bright.

Though what we have for now seems pale,
It's only for a little while;
We will be passing through the veil
To freedom from our present trial.

It's Jesus meets our every need,
Of all that is, the cornerstone;
For all our sakes to intercede,
He stands before the Father's throne.

His sacrifice made once for all,
The consummation is complete;
Onto our knees we can but fall,
Our empty crowns cast at His feet.

For Jesus turns the old to new,
Chains that once held us, cast aside;
New Earth, new Heaven pushing through,
He the groom, His Church the bride.

We wait in hope, stood on the verge,
From all that's past, He'll cut the cord:
Into His light we will emerge
To live forever with the Lord.

SONGS OF PERSPECTIVE

"But God said to him, 'You fool! This very night your life will be demanded from you. Then who will get what you have prepared for yourself?'..."

Luke 12:20

The last taboo?

Death is not a popular topic of conversation and for many remains unspoken; better to get on with life and not think about the inevitable (but hopefully far-off) prospect of it all coming to an end one day.

There are those who take comfort in the assumption that this life is all there is; that when you die, it is just as if someone switches off the light and there is no more: nothing beyond the grave.

While this might sit well with people who are disinterested in the things of God, it is not what the Bible tells us about life after death. Eternal life is for everyone (whether Christian or not): the key issue is how, where and with whom we will spend that eternity.

When we die, we will stand before God and be called to account for the life that we have lived. On our own, every one of us would be condemned for the sin that infects our lives, for we can never meet the standards of God's holiness. If we put our faith and trust in Jesus, however, he stands on our behalf before God, and through his perfect sacrifice made for us on the Cross he bore all the punishment that should be ours.

As Christians, we have the assurance that although we are 'broken' people (in the sense that we do wrong things in life), our entry to Heaven is secure because of Jesus defeating the power of sin and death and because he intervenes personally on our behalf.

In all things, there has to be balance: so it is with light and dark; whoever we are and however we have lived, we stand before God and face judgment when we die. The result will either be to enter the light of the eternal presence of God (Heaven) or the darkness of eternal separation from God (hell).

And we should have no doubt: the Bible makes it abundantly clear that 'hell' is not some vague metaphor for evil or darkness. It is a real place, a place where unending pain and torment will be played out in full, and from which there will be no escape or relief.

Which way this will go depends on the choice that we make while we still live. Life is fragile; and life may be (unexpectedly) cut short. None of us knows the hour of our dying and this brings sharply into focus the danger of putting off such a crucial decision.

For Christians, this life is a relatively brief interlude in the eternal scheme of things, where the greatest of joys we experience now can only ever be a pale reflection of the wonders that lie in store when God brings us home into Heaven. What a privilege to know that we will be welcomed into the Father's presence, as a forgiven and redeemed child of God.

Whatever our thoughts and beliefs about life and death, it is not uncommon at some time or another for people to have a sense of some inner prompting that whispers: 'there has to be more to life than this'.

Addressing this question cannot be avoided by simply doing nothing; not saying 'yes' to God is the same as saying 'no', with all the consequences which flow from such inaction.

Putting off a decision is a risky strategy: time is short – perhaps this is something at least worth exploring a bit more, while we still can…?

Last Day

If today was my last day, if I met You face to face,
Would I look You in the eye? Could I say I'd earned my place?
Could I point to all the ways that I had healed a broken heart,
Or had led the lost and lonely as they made a brand new start?
And could I say, with confidence, without the things I'd done
That so many, stood beside me, would have never known your Son?

If today was my last day, if I couldn't see tomorrow,
Would I search in desperation for some added time to borrow?
If I thought there'd be no more, would I find it so appalling
That I'd block my ears, to stop myself from hearing Jesus' calling?
Would I strain my every sinew, though I know what must be faced,
Too afraid I might discover that my hope had been misplaced?

If today was my last day, would I greet it as a friend,
Or a foe, to be resisted to a hard and bitter end?
If today was my last day, would I crave ten thousand more,
Or long, instead, to own the boundless joy that lies in store?
Could I treat this precious day as if it was, in truth, my last
Not yearning for forgotten time, lost long within my past?

If today was my last day, could I live it without fear,
Rejecting all those worldly things I'd held, too long, so dear?
If today was all remaining, would I cling to what I know
Or willingly relinquish all: at ease, and let it go?
Looking forward, would it be to me not final, but the first
Of the endless flow of Heaven's grace that satisfies all thirst?

If today was my last day, would I break into a smile;
So glad that I had stood the test and shared His every trial?
Would I put regret behind me, with the race already run:
Conformed, transformed forever, in the presence of your Son;
If tomorrow was an open door to all the wonders planned,
Would I be truly ready: in good conscience, could I stand?

When will I really count the cost? My final day, a treasure:
He breathed His last, to win for me new living, without measure!

We All Sleep

Too many, so determined to be masters of their fate,
Don't see the end approaching until it's far too late;
They think that by their gifts alone the present can be held,
But they will be uprooted, like a tree that must be felled;
Their time awake, for a short while, may seem to be a friend,
But still, the simple truth remains: we all sleep, in the end.

They build a reputation that they think will serve them well,
And if they harbour any doubts, they aren't about to tell;
They need nobody but themselves, secure in their success,
To be the first, to rule their world, accepting nothing less;
And yet the greatest climber from the heights must soon return,
Descending down an unmarked path, no bridges left to burn;
The things they valued most, now with so little to commend;
They see a truth they can't deny: we all sleep, in the end.

For all of those they pushed aside to scale each barren wall
Will stand as their accusers when the reaper comes to call;
What little credit they once had has swiftly drained away,
When called to give account, their empty profit holds no sway;
Backed into a dark corner they no longer can defend,
They face the truth that still remains: we all sleep, in the end.

But there is real awakening if we take another route,
If we throw in our cards and change into a different suit;
Exchanging rags for riches by confessing all our shame,
To clothe ourselves in righteousness by trust in Jesus' name,
Imbued by grace, with confidence the end is but the start,
To make a true connection with our loving Father's heart;
In hope and in humility, to let Him have His way:
Though we will sleep, our eyes will see a glorious new day.

Tipping Point

We're standing on the edge of time,
Expectant for the bell to chime:
The pealing of the final ring
That marks the end of everything.

In mercy, God has waited long
For all to raise a worship song,
To bow in awe, on bended knee:
Submission setting captives free.

But there will come a tipping point:
Each saint, in turn, God will anoint
For transformed life, in fullness lived,
The wheat from chaff forever sieved.

While those who are of different mind
Will reap the whirlwind, left behind;
Too late, they see they've lost the prize
That shone so bright before their eyes.
Their indecision ruled too long,
The time has passed to right the wrong,
Their chance is lost, the path is set,
That leads to only deep regret.

A sudden storm, the end appears:
The promise of so many years
Fulfilled, when He returns once more,
The chosen welcomed through the door
Receive their due, in at the birth
Of a new Heaven and new Earth.

This truth to us that's been unfurled
Needs sharing with a dying World:
There cannot be more urgent time,
Than when the bell's about to chime.

Last Throw of the Dice

This time will have an ending, though not ours to know the day,
When all will be remade by God, who has the final say;
The flavour of our fractured World is growing ever sour,
We look for new Creation, for the taste of God's great power.

Yet there remain so many, blissful ignorance their state,
Left to their own devices, won't awake till it's too late,
Their view of what is still to come seen like a distant moon;
Although it seems so far away, it will be coming soon.

The impact of just caring is beyond our means to tell,
The truth is ours for sharing and we have to do it well;
For God will honour every prayer that's raised to Him above,
That pleads for mercy for the lost and covers them with love.

We cannot waste a moment, when they may not be asked twice,
For what we say today could be the last throw of the dice;
And how we choose to play this hand should be of great concern,
For without further sixes rolled, there'll be no extra turn.

Though all is still to play for, there's an ending to the game,
With everything concluded, we will never be the same;
God's grace is offered freely, bought for all at such a cost,
But without true repentance, this great legacy is lost.

We can leave them in the darkness, with a future surely wrecked,
Or choose, instead, a better way, our Saviour's love reflect,
To bring them revelation of the One who truly cares:
Turn losers into winners, so the victory, too, is theirs.

SONGS OF REDEMPTION

---

*"I am the Alpha and the Omega," says the Lord God, "who is,
and who was, and who is to come, the Almighty."*

Revelation 1:8

Alpha and Omega... it is finished

The focus on Christmas as the key Christian festival may give the impression that this is the high (and only really significant) point in the Christian calendar; and that other, lesser, festivals such as Easter, are merely poor cousins to be noted only in passing.

But while it is undoubtedly good to celebrate long and loud the birth of the Saviour of the World (albeit probably, historically, on the wrong date!), it is not so much how he started, but rather how he concluded, his time on Earth that truly holds the key to our eternal future.

Spiritually, we are broken people and the World we inhabit is broken too. But the good news is that God has the tools to fix the problem and that, at that first Easter, he initiated a unique and perfectly flawless repair plan.

Our modern sensibilities can make us struggle with the reality of the Cross; we would rather not think about the unpalatable and shocking truth of what Jesus endured, in sacrificing himself by submitting to one of the most horrific forms of execution known to the ancient world.

But it is on the Cross that the most profound and mysterious transaction was made, with Jesus taking upon himself the punishment that is rightly ours; and, in doing so, breaking forever the power of sin and death over our lives and opening up for us the way to a new, eternal, life with God.

Life goes on forever. The question for everyone is a stark one: Heaven or hell; light or dark. Where and how – and with whom – will we choose to spend that eternity?

There is only one way to God…

Repair Man

Called out on a whim, the repair man is hailed
As the one who can 'fix it' – the problem's been nailed,
So they think – but as quickly their Saviour rejected,
When they see that the task is not what they expected.

All that they had constructed, considered complete:
Their fear is it all will crash down at their feet,
As He seeks to rebuild something far beyond man,
To restore the designer's original plan.

Only He has the tools that can finish the job,
Dispensing such love in the face of a mob
Who are braying and hostile, who seek to destroy
All He longs to make new with an infinite joy.

Only He knows the way, when we're falling to pieces,
To make us anew, ironing out all the creases;
He comes to restore, in His glory and grace,
A temple much more than a physical space.

"He is nothing!" they cry, and they think He must fail
In the face of the heartless misuse of the nail;
As the hammer blows fall, as they see His blood run,
"Let him tend to himself, if he's really the one."

Determined, they break every sinew and bone
With each splinter and crack a more terrible moan;
His anguish exceeding the most we could bear,
Enduring for us, for our perfect repair.

In the end, it is finished, the job is complete
As the nails are removed from His hands and His feet;
As He's shrouded, entombed, though the task seems undone,
In a matter of days, He will rise with the Sun.

Confirming the wonder of which He had spoken,
Renewed and remade, He can never be broken.
So we are reborn, through this love without measure:
New life, freely given, our true Easter treasure.

Friday Sacrifice

Today, we focus on the Cross,
His sacrifice, His dying;
When Jesus chose to bear our loss
In deepest self-denying.

He hung, alone, in agony,
Weighed heavy by our sinning;
Throughout the darkest of all days,
Our good forever winning.

He paid our dues in full for us,
More than we could afford;
The debt completely settled
By the mercy of the Lord.

Though none could take His life away,
He was not slow to give it;
He bought for us eternal life
That we might fully live it.

He finished what He started,
What He'd always come to do;
The task was His alone,
For no one else could see it through.

He could have faltered, turned aside,
But love compelled His giving
Of all He had; and so, He died,
Brought low, yet raised to living.

Good Friday's suffering makes us pause,
Enveloped by the night;
But Easter Sunday's promise points us
To salvation's light.

A glory that outshines the gloom
Of Friday's darkest hour;
The Lord's undying love revealed
In all its might and power.

Without the Friday sacrifice
Of God's anointed Son,
The victory of the empty tomb
Would never have been won.

Because of His great love for us,
We're raised on Heaven's wings.
Let's praise Him now, and ever more,
New life His dying brings!

Easter Rising

I sat outside the empty tomb,
Stone moved, the body gone;
No longer shrouded deep in gloom,
Now only daylight shone.
And, sitting next to Jesus
On that glorious Easter Day,
The silence spoke in volumes,
As He had the final say.

I knew He'd gained the victory,
To spare my dying shame,
He didn't say a single word,
Yet still He called my name;
There was no need to speak at all,
His radiance filled my heart,
Content that there was nothing left
For keeping us apart.

The awesomeness of all He'd done,
Too much to comprehend:
He bought me sweet beginnings
From a hard and bitter end;
And I, so glad that He would share
His resurrection light,
In love, that He arrayed me
In His robes of perfect white.

The stormy oceans I once sailed
With constant ebb and flow,
Now, put aside, the ups and downs
Of every high and low;
Instead, with true contentment
To be sitting at His side,
The graveclothes gone, discarded,
As His rising turned the tide.

I felt a strange elation,
My heart was fit to burst,
Where once I might have doubted,
Now I knew He put me first.
And so, the song I'm singing
Has a wholly new refrain;
From all my Saviour chose to lose
I've everything to gain.
Though not the end of death itself,
His rising breaks its power:
Easter brings a glorious Spring,
New life into full flower!

Songs of Salvation

...when the kindness and love of God our Saviour appeared, he saved us, not because of righteous things we had done, but because of his mercy. He saved us through the washing of rebirth and renewal by the Holy Spirit, whom he poured out on us generously through Jesus Christ our Saviour...

Titus 3:4-6

An unexpected rescue plan

Humanly speaking, the Christmas story presents us with a problem: an immaculate conception and a virgin birth?!

To the modern reader, this seems implausible to say the least, and perhaps even a little ridiculous.

But if there is a God who made the Universe and who holds all of his Creation in place, then it is perfectly reasonable to assume that someone with such ultimate authority and power can, should he choose, do things which defy the 'laws of nature' as we understand them; not least, because he made those laws!

And who else but God could have come up with such an extraordinary and unexpected rescue plan to deal with the deadly legacy of sin in all of our lives?

Instead of questioning his methods, we should surely be expressing our unending gratitude and thankfulness for a God whose selfless actions are motivated by a readiness to forgive and to be merciful, in spite of the rejection and disbelief that all too often characterise our own selfish attitudes and behaviour.

It is a joy indeed to know that the King is come!

Rescue

We're lost, adrift on stormy seas,
Our frail ship is tossed and turned.
The waves are raging, never ease,
It's nothing less than we have earned.

For setting sail upon a course
Without a hand to guide the way
Exposes us to deadly force,
Where hope is sinking, day by day.

We've seen it many times before,
When on our own we plough ahead,
The captain waiting on the shore,
Our confidence is left for dead.

To think that we could walk upon
The water, buoyed by foolish pride,
Our self-assurance quickly gone,
The sea pours in on every side.

It's only when we let Him steer,
The tiller held in His sure hand,
That we can be relieved of fear,
To reach a safer place to land.

The weight of all our failings drags,
For only He can make it right,
He takes away our filthy rags,
Replacing them with robes of white.

It's when true rescue can begin,
Let none deny, let no one doubt:
We're all in the same boat of sin,
God's grace alone can bail us out.

The Light

The star came to rest, two millennia past,
Overcoming the shadows the night had once cast;
The sign in the sky a new message imparted,
That something unique and amazing had started.

Creation rejoiced when the baby was born,
Announcing new life on that first Christmas morn;
The heavens were filled with unending refrain
That the dark that once held us could no longer reign.

The star, in its radiance, blazing like fire,
The flames had been fanned that would never expire;
A million suns but a flickering glow,
When compared to that light in the stable below.

Its gleaming outshining the embers of doubt,
It cannot be extinguished or ever go out;
We're no longer consumed by the pall of the night,
With a torch for the present, our future lit bright.

From the humblest of starts, God's incredible plan,
Our hearts were illumed, as our rescue began;
Jesus shines with a love only He can display,
Igniting a truth that has shown us the way.

The darkness defeated, we bathe in His light
That cleanses our souls and will robe us in white,
In a dazzling array beyond anything known,
On that glorious day when He makes us His own!

Against All Odds

By many You were spoken of unkindly,
It seemed to them You rolled the dice so blindly;
But You resolved to heed your Father's leading,
New life assured, just as the old was bleeding,
That there was greater profit from obeying,
Submitting to God's will in all your praying.

Though it would be so easy to forsake it,
You saw the road ahead, yet chose to take it;
An ending that could not have been more shocking
Would open up the path sin had been blocking.

Against all odds, by trusting in God's leading,
Your very life prepared to be conceding,
The most unlikely victory You were winning,
To bring us, in the end, to new beginning.

Against all odds, the barriers are broken
As mercy from the throne of Heaven is spoken.
Your lifeless body in a cold tomb waiting
For resurrection power, anticipating;
And as the breath of God came swiftly flowing,
The flower of new life in full bloom growing.

The mockers left to wonder how such giving
Could pave the way for our eternal living,
Not comprehending faith calls for deciding:
That once the die is cast, there is no hiding.

Against all odds, the power of death defeated,
The prince of darkness from his throne unseated;
On worldly powers bringing down the curtain,
A victory that once had seemed uncertain
Was now delivered in the strangest fashion,
By Jesus' love, obedience, and compassion.

Once

Your dying was a one-time thing,
your rising was the same;
You set the canvas of our lives
Into a different frame.

Your sacrifice was once for all
That never needs repeating,
The power of darkness swept away,
All empty thrones unseating.

The transformation made complete:
Once done, forever finished;
The guarantee of life renewed
Can never be diminished.

Forever drawn, the sting of death,
Its fear no longer pains us;
Your Holy Spirit fills our hearts,
Once breathed, and now sustains us.

Your dying once means we will live,
Your rising brings salvation;
It all is done, we are remade:
Your glorious new Creation!

SONGS OF SERVANTHOOD

[Jesus said] "…whoever wants to become great among you must be your servant, and whoever wants to be first must be slave of all. For even the Son of Man did not come to be served, but to serve, and to give his life as a ransom for many."

Mark 10:43-45

The servant king

When Jesus is referred to as a 'servant king', we are presented with an uncomfortable paradox. If he is our king, then surely it should be we who serve him, not the other way around?

We are indeed called to serve him, not least by treating him with the awe and respect that he deserves and by praising and exalting his name in all we say and do.

But Jesus made it abundantly clear during his time on Earth that, in the most practical way possible, we can serve him best when we render service to other people. In this sense, we are to be his hands and his feet, giving others the same care, time and attention that we seek for ourselves, and in doing so showing his love to those around us.

What does this service look like?

It means putting others' needs ahead of our own; making their priorities our priorities; helping them to find the best of themselves and walking with them in sharing their ups and downs, their highs and lows; and helping to steer them towards a sense of true fulfilment and contentment through trust in Jesus.

This calls for insight, discernment and a large dose of empathy on our part; and it will most likely also require us to make (perhaps significant) personal sacrifices.

Finding ourselves living in a society that seems to be forever focussed on the 'me' – how can I get what I want to make me happy – the challenge for Christians is to be intentionally different; to be counter-cultural, ready to endure and overcome the dismissal of an unbelieving World, and to shine Jesus' light into otherwise spiritually dark places.

Far from being thought of as a burden, it is our greatest privilege and joy to serve forever the One who made each of us and all of Creation.

Servant Feet

To look to others' needs and not our own,
Begins to show how much our love has grown;
In serving those we know, and those to meet,
We'll be content to take the lowest seat.

If Jesus would be servant of us all,
We cannot rest, forever standing tall;
His call to follow cannot be denied:
We have to cast our selfish ways aside.

To kneel where Jesus' love and mercy meet,
Prepared to daily wash a stranger's feet,
To show God's grace to all He longs to know,
Will see a wave of transformation flow.

And through the great exemplar of God's love,
Our eyes may turn from us, to look above;
Discovering humility that's true,
To serve, exalting Him in all we do.

First

When all of my ambition had been focussed on the prize,
My self-appreciation I could not cut down to size;
It seemed my role to reach the top was constantly rehearsed
In a World that shouts so loudly: 'There's only coming first!'

Yet, something still was missing and just waiting to be found:
I hoped that I would grasp it as I reached for higher ground;
For I had been left high and dry and had not quenched my thirst,
In seeking elevation and in putting myself first.

Chasing after rainbows that I thought I must deserve
Had only thrown me from my path into an endless curve;
With winning all that mattered, the spotlight shone on me,
I lost all sense of who it was that I was made to be.
The confidence I thought would raise me to the greatest height
Had led me to a place which saw my disappointment bite;
The emptiness of wealth and fame, the bubble set to burst,
The lustre quickly fading from the lure of being first.

The trail that I'd pursued so long was slowly going cold,
My thoughts turned to how differently my life might yet unfold;
For seeking after number one had only left me cursed:
I had to find another way, not putting myself first.

God chose to be the least of us: though worthy of a throne,
He came to serve our every need and sacrificed His own;
Through grace, in deep humility, He made our roles reversed
And gave of everything He had, resolved to put me first.

With all I'd known turned on its head, my time to break the past,
To stand aside, content to be exchanging first for last;
To learn from Him the virtues of a truly servant heart:
It's when I choose the lowest place my rise can truly start.

The World may shout, but God's soft voice is drowning out the noise,
The empty sounds, that once held sway, salvation's song destroys;
Although among the sinners I may be ranked with the worst,
I still can find true living when I put my Saviour first.

His Hands and Feet

Jesus heals, because He can,
So far beyond the wit of man;
Yet He invites us to join in,
For deeper healing of our sin.
The darkness flees, in full retreat,
When we, as Jesus' hands and feet
By faith, are vessels of His power,
His love on those in need to shower.

We sense the wind of change begin:
The Kingdom come, is breaking in,
Where grace, and love, and mercy meet,
Where we, as Jesus' hands and feet,
Walk in His ways and draw the lost
To recognise He paid the cost,
So they could be forever free,
Restored as they were made to be.

Alone, we're little more than fools,
Yet He equips us with the tools,
Though our own strength is in retreat,
Still we become His hands and feet;
He lifts us from the rank and file
So we may go the extra mile;
Dispensing comfort, love and care,
As if the Lord is standing there.

So, Jesus heals, because He can,
And we, submitting to His plan,
Our hungry souls, He fully feeds,
We follow where the Spirit leads;
Surrendering the hour each day,
Content for Him to have His way:
This great assurance for the soul,
That He alone is in control.

Rise

The wisdom of the years has found,
To keep our feet upon the ground,
Not craving greater heights instead,
Is how to follow all He said.

We do not have to climb across
The wasteland of another's loss,
Indifferent to all their pain,
For us to grab the highest gain.

He bids us walk a different way,
In servanthood, to win the day;
Our pride and envy in retreat,
Content to have the lowest seat.

While those on top have far to fall,
Our place, the very least of all;
We settle for the servant's cup,
Assured that He will lift us up.

We know it was for this He died,
To see a pattern override;
To spark a change in human hearts,
That brings the greatest of new starts.

This truth, we surely should have learned
Our place in Heaven can't be earned:
For Jesus has already won
A place for us, by all He's done.

We serve, responding to His grace,
The lowest seat the highest place;
We need to look for no reward,
Than giving glory to the Lord;
This is the greatest prize of all:
To rise with Him and never fall.

SONGS OF SUBMISSION

Although he was a son, [Jesus] learned obedience from what he suffered and, once made perfect, he became the source of eternal salvation for all who obey him...

Hebrews 5:8-9

Submit yourselves, then, to God. Resist the devil, and he will flee from you. Come near to God and he will come near to you... Humble yourselves before the Lord, and he will lift you up.

James 4:7-8, 10

Following the leader

The idea of 'submission' can carry negative connotations, suggesting that we must give up something to which we think we are entitled, or that we will have to make ourselves subservient to another's will.

To the modern ear, this goes against the grain of our sensibilities about personal liberty and freedom of action.

However, there is a world of difference between restrictions imposed with a view to forcing people to bend to another's will or a particular way of thinking, as opposed to the setting of sensible and reasoned boundaries and safeguards that are put in place with the benefit of all in mind.

The Bible is not some harsh rulebook designed to inhibit our enjoyment of life. On the contrary, the principles and guidelines that it contains are there to protect us from ourselves, from unnecessary harm that might otherwise ensue when we recklessly pursue our own agenda, without thought for the consequences.

Jesus is the ultimate example of submission; obediently deferring to the will of his Father, in the absolute confidence that God knows what is best for us.

God is always looking out for our physical, emotional and spiritual wellbeing. Given his credentials, perhaps insisting on having our own way in all things is not such a smart approach after all.

Can we really afford to ignore his leading…?

Exalted

Sat on my throne of possessions and wealth,
My pride in a life in the rudest of health,
Thinking that nothing can topple my rule,
Not seeing my wisdom as that of a fool;
I'm blinkered and missing what's truly of worth:
Content with a place that's exalted on Earth.

Too easy to cling to the things I can see,
With a future depending entirely on me;
How am I so blind that I'm still yet to learn,
That all I possess and the more that I earn,
Secure for me nothing but chaff turned to dust,
Blown on the wind of a vacuous trust?

The richest of men, yet the poorest in soul,
For all that I gather will not make me whole;
Of my empty existence, the truth slowly dawning:
Gone, in an instant, without any warning.

If the lilies are clothed and the birds are all fed,
How much more will my Saviour provide me with bread?
When I know He is giving me all, and much more,
Reassured that He only has good things in store;
And if want is my meal in the days to be mine,
For my sake, He will put all He has on the line.

My hope should be raised to the greatest of height,
In walking with Jesus by faith, not by sight;
The things of this World, paled and fading from view,
As I trust in His power to remake and renew.

Accepting His grace and the promised new birth,
At last, I might see what is truly of worth:
To be raised up with Him, not exalted on Earth.

To the Moon and Back

In times when so much pride in worldly wisdom is at large,
Too easily we fool ourselves that we have taken charge;
Our knowledge so developed, our genius in play,
That if we put our minds to it, then we will win the day;
That we need nothing greater than the light of our own star,
The kings of all that we survey is surely who we are;
We think it undeniable, the truth we're pushing through:
'Now we've been to the Moon and back, there's nothing we can't do!'

So much that we have overcome, succumbing to our will,
Our certainty in who we are runs into overspill;
We marvel how we've come so far from origins so small,
That now we have complete control, we need no help at all.
Our reach is all-encompassing, there's nothing out of range,
While every aspect of our lives is ours to freely change;
An arrogance that knows no bounds, dismissing every test:
'Since we've been to the Moon and back, we're sure that we know best'.

But when the unexpected out of left field takes a bow,
That undermines our future and disrupts the here and now,
We find ourselves so ill-equipped, our efforts come to naught,
And having overplayed our hand, no longer holding court,
The walls of our defences breached, we cannot hide the cracks,
Revealing shallow confidence and just how much it lacks;
We're left with only questions, so unsure of where we are:
'Though we've been to the Moon and back, perhaps this is too far'.

If there was not a different path that we could choose to follow,
Such doses of reality would be too hard to swallow;
But God knows all our failings and He hears us when we pray,
If earnestly we look to Him, to find another way,
Acknowledging in Him alone that we can have our fill;
When we in true humility submit to Jesus' will,
Then we can join Creation's song, assured that all is true:
'Our Lord's been to the grave and back: there's nothing He can't do'.

Reliance

Too often I feel like I'm weak as a mouse,
That hides in the dark in the bowels of the house;
Caught underfoot in the light of the day,
With the cat on the prowl, I do not get to play.

When I think that I'm safe and cannot be pursued,
That I need no one's help to secure my own food,
Forgetting it's God who is bridging the gap:
It's then that I find myself caught in the trap.

If I open my eyes to the truth that I know,
Equipped by the Lord, with His grace in full flow,
No longer against me, the tides that I swim,
My weakness made strong, through submission to Him;
My reliance on God the true mark of my trust,
With my strength put aside, trodden deep in the dust.

When the gratitude's mine, and He has all the glory,
When it's all about Him and His salvation story;
When the World sees such good that is truly achieved,
As we give Him control, as His Word is believed;
When they see He is constant and won't let us fall,
They may come to believe that He cares for us all.

Every victory won, every point that is scored,
Let us give all the credit that's due to the Lord;
While the World might still see me as feeble and weak,
Though it's my voice that's heard, may they hear Jesus speak.

Reaching for the Moon

The greatest prize of all cannot be gained by our endeavour,
It matters not how much our wit, our guile, or being clever;
Though reaching for the Moon, too soon we tumble to the Earth,
To find that, on their own, our efforts are of little worth.

We cannot find the truth while holed up in our ivory tower,
So soon run out of steam when we are fuelled by our own power;
Our confidence in our own might, the rightness of our thinking,
Will leave us running high and dry, from stagnant water drinking.

The prize remains for winning, in a wholly new direction,
For God is there to steer us, as we reach the intersection;
The plans that we're adopting must be only of His making,
Mapped out in full relief, we see the route we should be taking.

The destination looming, we may have to wait to enter,
For He decides who's going first, who's standing at the centre;
It matters not who takes the lead, and who is in the chorus,
Content to wait, to stand aside, let others go before us;
Our search for elevation counterbalanced by the notion
That being His gatekeeper is the greatest of promotion.

If, without Him, we try to see the way the land is lying,
We'll never head to Heaven's shore, no matter all our trying;
Our reaching for the Moon may be the loftiest ambition,
But, without God as pilot, it will be a fruitless mission.

SONGS OF TRANSFORMATION

Do not conform any longer to the pattern of this world, but be transformed by the renewing of your mind. Then you will be able to test and approve what God's will is – his good, pleasing and perfect will.

Romans 12:2

Ringing the changes

Have you ever found yourself wondering what life is really for? Why are we here?

However physically healthy, materially prosperous, or career-successful we may be, it is not uncommon for most of us at some time or other in our lives to experience a sense of something missing: is this all there is, or is there something more?

Without being able to form a clear sense of what this might be, and while struggling to put this into words, we can find ourselves searching for something that seems both tantalisingly close, while at the same time just out of reach: something that could bring a real sense of fulfilment and completion, if we could just take hold of it.

As Christians, we believe that we are made to be in a living relationship with our Creator and that only God can fill the emptiness in our souls, of which we become increasingly aware as we continue to live our lives apart from him.

Allowing him to shape who we are can be a truly life-transforming experience.

Is it time for a change?

Someone Else?

When I'm alone, I find him there,
Sitting with me, in my chair;
And strange ideas caress his mind,
To which my self is often blind.

His promises are all my hope,
With my fool's fears he seems to cope;
The dreams I shun, though wish as true
Are then rekindled, full, anew.

He vows that we will walk as one,
To smash the shell that hides the Sun;
To break life's long and languid course,
And brim instead with all its force.

A man of instinct, wild and free,
He yet remains a part of me;
But when, at last, I leave the chair,
Alas! He is no longer there.

In My Own World

I used to live in my own world, so easy to inhabit,
Where, craving anything I'd want, I only had to grab it;
I used to give no second thought to anything but me,
The centre of my universe was where I longed to be.
I used to think the axis around which my world rotated
Would turn out to be all I want, my hunger fully sated;
It used to be about my needs, all else had been forsaken:
My confidence in my own way was never to be shaken.

I used to stand atop my world as if upon a throne,
Believing all that I achieved had been my very own;
And I would boast that everything that I had ever learned
Was surely wrought by my strong arm, the help of others spurned.

I used to think I held the key, unlocking every door,
That I alone was in control of all that lay in store;
I used to think the more I tried, the more I would succeed,
That following the path I'd forged would meet my every need.
I used to think the answers laid entirely in my hand,
That everything would come to pass exactly as I'd planned.

Yet rounds of disappointment, and of striving without end,
Revealed my self-absorption as a frail and fickle friend;
It took so long to realise the truth from which I'd hidden,
That all the good You had for me my pride had overridden;
But when I let your Spirit speak and turned my ear for hearing,
I sensed the World I thought I knew might yet be disappearing.

Where once I only looked to fight and never dared to waver,
Your love revealed I didn't have to earn a single favour;
You opened up my eyes to see that following your leading,
Surrendering my will to yours, You meet my every needing.
Instead of chasing empty dreams, I've found a winning cause:
I used to live in my own world: but now, I'm seeking yours.

Changed

There'll come a day when every eye
Will see God's glory raised on high;
The fullness of His power displayed,
    When everything will be remade.

    While longing to be on our way,
    To hear the final trumpet play,
The ring of change so sweetly chiming,
We wait, our trust in His good timing.

But change has not been put on hold,
    We must not let the food grow cold:
    He calls us more than merely taste,
The feast He serves not put to waste.
    For, even in this waiting hour,
    We are connected by His power,
    The Spirit living in our hearts
That bids us make the best of starts.

His Kingdom seen not fully yet,
But His deliverance has been set;
So many seeds still to be sown,
And by His hand we'll see them grown.

In knowing we are not forsaken,
Our confidence cannot be shaken;
Because He lives, because He died,
We stand forgiven, sanctified.

And when the present time has burned,
We'll leave, and then will be returned,
Remade, reborn, and clothed anew,
Death cannot stop our passing through.
His sacrifice and endless grace
Will lead us to our resting place;
Brought home, at last, secure and free,
Transformed to who we're made to be.

Though much, it seems, is yet unchanged,
Until the World is rearranged
Our call remains to spread the word,
For faith takes root where truth is heard;
To point towards the coming King,
And the salvation He will bring.
He promises an open door,
Yet what He brings is so much more:
Such depths of love we've yet to plumb,
The greatest change is still to come!

Miracle in Me (a song)

Though faith can move a mountain
Only you can change my heart
Your grace is like a fountain
You take my pride apart.
To break and recreate me
Old living washed aside,
A wave of mercy rising
That forever turns the tide:

Chorus

You've made a miracle in me
The mountains move apart and fall into the sea
Consuming love flows like a flood
And by your precious blood
I am set free:
You've made a miracle, a miracle in me

Though faith can move a mountain
Only you can lead me in
Immerse me in your fountain
And wipe away my sin.
You take a broken pattern
Restoring your design,
To change and rearrange me,
So your righteousness is mine:

Chorus

Though faith can move a mountain
Only you can see me through
Washed clean beneath your fountain
Transformed from old to new.
You bring it all together
Held by your mighty hand,
To be with you forever;
By your sweet grace I will stand:

Chorus

SONGS OF TRUTH

Jesus said…, "I am the resurrection and the life. He who believes in me will live, even though he dies; and whoever lives and believes in me will never die…".

John 11:25

A truth that can be trusted

We are sometimes told that there are two kinds of truth: subjective truth – what someone chooses to believe despite any supporting proof; and objective truth – belief based upon independently verifiable evidence.

There is a strong correlation between belief and truth. Simply deciding to believe something without any basis in observable reality might be thought of as little more than delusion. Wanting something to be true does not make it true.

Christianity stands or falls upon whether or not the resurrection of Jesus actually happened. A belief is vindicated when it is shown to be based on objective truth; and so it is, with the Christian faith.

Applying the commonly-accepted standards of proof upon which the veracity of all secular history is evaluated, the historical proof for the life, death and in particular the resurrection of Jesus, as portrayed in the Bible, might arguably be said to have been established beyond reasonable doubt. There is no space here to consider the array of available evidence; but there are many published books that have been written on the subject, that are available to help explore this further.

As humans, we all have a limited 'shelf life'. While our time on Earth continues, we occupy perishable mortal bodies which are destined to fail, sooner or later.

The qualitative difference with the risen Jesus is that he no longer inhabits the frail mortal body that was previously his. He was resurrected: in a recognisable, but wholly new and imperishable body, lasting through all eternity. Christians look forward to the same. This fundamental truth is central to the Christian faith.

The resurrection of Jesus was a once and for all, one-off event.

Jesus' death and resurrection is what assures us that sin and death no longer have power over us; that we can freely receive the forgiveness of all our failings before God; and that we are guaranteed eternal life with him.

Why is the resurrection story, for so many, so hard to swallow? The elephant in the room is that we have to be able to look past our narrow Earthly perspective; it calls for us to be open to and accept the possibility of something supernatural, beyond our normal everyday worldly experience.

Have we for so long existed on a diet that is so limited to such a small part of all that life really has to offer, that the flavour of a deeper truth simply gets missed and is never tasted?

True History

We read of ages past, of distant lives,
Though just a written fragment still survives,
That all these things occurred we take as read,
And rarely doubt what ancient writers said.

But when it comes to something so profound,
When we are called to stand on holy ground,
Accepting that a man who surely died
Came back to life, and cast the stone aside,
Though by all normal measures it is clear,
And must be true, we cannot shake the fear
Of having to concede there may be more
Than everything that we believed before.

Although it takes a supernatural twist,
It doesn't mean reality is missed;
For if it really happened – and it did –
Today must be the time to lift the lid.
It's not on wishful thinking that it rests,
The facts to which the evidence attests
In any other setting would be seen
As confirmation just how things had been

And everyone who tries to prove it wrong
Has found they must give up before too long;
Their efforts to deny instead have shown
This is a truth that no one should disown.

There is a hope on which we can rely:
The end is the beginning when we die;
The greatest story will not go away,
The truth of Jesus Christ is here to stay.

Remade

When we have left this place behind, departing life's last station,
Our hearts will fill with joy to reach the perfect destination;
Like waiting for some great event, we can't be more excited
Than when our Saviour calls us home, when every wrong is righted.

This will not be the life we knew, not just a version better,
But something far beyond our hopes, removing every fetter
That once had held us in its grasp, now gone; there's no mistaking
That nothing will be as it was – for us, complete remaking;
Our unfulfilled desires met, with His, our hearts, aligning,
The longings that we knew before now to the past consigning.

We'll recognise the saints we knew, yet differently related,
For in this new existence we are wholly recreated;
Our bodies made entirely new, and fit to last forever,
All struggle long forgotten now, His praise our one endeavour.

With all renewed, our souls are given freely in surrender,
As Jesus draws us home, we will be clothed in holy splendour;
His love, that is enduring and extending beyond measure:
We'll have no need for more than this: our God, eternal treasure.

The Illusion of Truth

We've allowed ourselves the illusion of untruth for far too long,
Too easily convinced that there is nothing we've done wrong;
That, sheltered from the storms, the rains that fall can never soak us,
Our hearts and minds are blinded by a flood of hocus-pocus.

When something's said so often, it's too easy to believe it,
Although the truth is lurking, we too often don't perceive it;
But there's no magic bullet for this tricky situation,
We can't just wave a wand to fix this mess of our creation.

We think we have it in ourselves to overcome each hurdle,
That we will never see our little good begin to curdle,
That there is nothing going bad, that all is in our favour:
Believing that defeat is not a taste we have to savour.

We're choosing to ignore our sheer perversity of action,
We fail to see the darker side of us is gaining traction;
For when we're riding roughshod, lacking any sense of feeling,
The fate we don't see taking hold will soon be set for sealing.

Though everything has come apart, we carry on, unthinking,
We're pouring out a bitter cup that we just can't stop drinking;
The well's become unusable, beyond recourse, and tainted:
Into a corner of regret that we ourselves have painted.

Though God has shown the change we need, if we go on resisting,
To suit our way of thinking weave a truth we won't stop twisting,
There's only condemnation that awaits at every turning:
The gap grows ever wider, with each bridge that we are burning.

Yet even standing on the brink, our Saviour, still, is calling,
To save us from ourselves, from an alternative appalling;
The choice, though, is for us to make, free given and sincerely,
It has to be wholehearted, there is never room for nearly.

It's only by a contrite heart, surrendered so completely,
That we can join the choirs of Heaven, forever singing sweetly;
When the illusion's overcome, when heavy scales are falling,
It's then that we might see the way, responding to His calling,
And wonder how we'd closed our hearts to everything He gave us:
For it is only Jesus' love that has the power to save us.

SONGS FOR A TIME YET TO COME
PART 2: THE ETERNAL GOD

SONGS OF CONTEMPLATION

"...Be still, and know that I am God..."

Psalm 46:10

[Jesus said] "Come to me, all you who are weary and burdened, and I will give you rest."

Matthew 11:28

Taking a breath

Deadlines: these days it seems to be all about deadlines. 'How soon?' is too often a loaded question, not infrequently carrying with it a wholly unreasonable expectation of almost instant results.

The World is full of so much hurrying, that continually wears us down.

Just as with the provision of retail and other services, we can become all too easily programmed to look for same-day or, at least, next-day delivery in all areas of our lives: in our work; in our leisure; in our relationships.

But all this rushing comes at a price; taking a toll on our physical, mental and spiritual wellbeing. We are so consumed by the need to keep up with the many competing demands on our time, that we can fill our days with too much 'doing', without ever taking stock or finding time to contemplate what all this frantic activity is really achieving.

In the Bible, God invites people to rest in him, to slow down, to put aside the worries of the day and to make space to spend time in his presence; in short, simply to 'be'.

We need to get our priorities right; we need to be intentional in building intervals into our busy day when we can just stop, rest in quiet contemplation, and seek to hear what God might be saying to us.

Perhaps there will never be a better time than now for a change of pace and for the discovery of new rhythms and healthier patterns of living.

Do we want to spend our precious time simply running, just to stand still? Or will we let ourselves draw breath, while we still have some air left to breathe?

Stop

Sometimes, I think, God just wants us to stop,
To take stock of our lives, look for what we might drop;
Ponder all that's important, and what we don't need;
To allow just a little more time to be freed,
To give ourselves space, just to listen and learn
From the still, smaller, voice that will call us to turn
To the way of the Spirit that dwells in our heart;
To draw close and stop holding ourselves far apart.

For it's only in Him that we find true release
From the burdens that stop us enjoying His peace,
And the glare of the World will be faded and dim
If we put all aside that distracts us from Him,
If we sit at His feet in reverence and awe,
Consumed by a longing to praise and adore.

If our heart and our mind truly seek Him alone,
If we fall to our knees at His glorious throne,
If we bow to His will, letting Him take the lead:
When we let ourselves stop, He will meet every need.

To rest in His presence, He wants us to pray
For His Spirit to guide at the start of each day.
Though we offer so little, His grace will abound:
It's our stopping that leads us to God's higher ground.

Just Look Up

God's goodness in abundance
Fills my overflowing cup;
I wait in silence, awestruck,
As He bids me: 'just look up'.

The hold of sin is broken,
The darkness has been riven;
I wait in silent reverence,
As He says: 'you are forgiven'.

A light forever shining,
All His glory fills the skies;
I wait in silent wonder,
As He calls to me: 'arise!'

My one response, to worship,
Onto my knees to fall;
I wait in silence, humbled,
As He says: 'you are my all!'

His love poured in abundance
Fills my overflowing cup;
I wait in silence, hands raised,
Gaze transfixed, and just look up.

Small Voice

Sometimes, I don't know where I should begin,
When all the noise of living hems me in;
The power of my praying seems so weak,
I wonder, will I ever hear God speak?

Though signs and wonders sometimes may be seen,
In truth, these can be few and far between;
To yearn for the spectacular and grand
Will just distract from all that He has planned.

The loudest shout will never win the day,
When quiet whispers have so much to say;
To set all else aside should be my choice,
Anticipate the sweetness of His voice.
The silence won't be deafening to Him,
My empty glass filled fully, to the brim;
With all He has to share resounding clear,
His words of love and comfort draw me near.

So, if I seek His rest, and still my heart,
To set some truly quiet time apart,
My listening soul may flower to full bloom,
To hear the echo of the empty tomb,
A power that inhabits every word,
So nothing that He says remains unheard.

This should be all my seeking, to the end,
With quiet contemplation as my friend,
His small, calm, voice is all I long to hear,
Speaking volumes, gently, in my ear.

Waiting

When I fail to seek the Lord,
To move within His sweet accord,
When I fail to seek His will,
I only taste the bitter pill
Of half found life, of hope unmet,
Of 'might have been' and sad regret.

Too often, human patience strains
To loose me from imagined chains,
As if the rush to all I seek
Will bring me to some lofty peak.
Instead, it only lays me low,
Confined within the things I know.

Forged on well-intentioned haste,
Through endless miles of fruitless waste,
So keen to be the one that wins,
I've lost before the day begins;
I take a route that's not been set
And wonder why I'm not home yet.

Sometimes, I'm called to walk, not run,
Or wait, though others have begun;
I cannot hope to win the race,
By charging on at frantic pace;
Of all direction, losing sense,
I only see a future, tense.

My frenzied dash brings no escape,
I crash, exhausted, through the tape
That wins for me a scant reward,
An emptiness, without the Lord.

His word drowned out, I cannot hear,
Although I know He's standing near;
I sense a voice within me say:
'There has to be a better way'.

If I but waited at His feet
In silence, there my Lord to meet,
Humility to fill my core,
To claim His promise from before;
If I could let impatience die
And just accept, not question why.

If I could seek His loving smile
And sit, just for a little while;
To bathe within His warming glow,
To hear the things He bids me know.

If I could put away my pride,
Accepting there's no need to hide,
Made perfect by His gift for me,
The promise of eternity;
I'd only want to seek His will,
Instead of mine, and hold so still,
The quiet of His Spirit's shade
Would hold me fast, to be remade:

Perhaps, at last, I'd finally hear, the voice that takes away all fear.

SONGS OF CREATION

[Christ] is the image of the invisible God, the firstborn over all creation. For by him all things were created: things in heaven and on earth, visible and invisible, whether thrones or powers or rulers or authorities; all things were created by him and for him. He is before all things, and in him all things hold together.

Colossians 1:15-17

Creation calls

God is a creative God. When he had finished putting into place the Universe in all its beauty and diversity, the Bible – in a wonderfully understated way – tells us that 'God saw all that he had made, and it was very good' (Genesis 1:31).

God has made a world of great wonder; a world of infinite variety, colour and texture; a world of extraordinary beauty. This is surely something that everyone should nurture and cherish. We should never forget that we are a part of God's Creation, not apart from it.

Yet God took the remarkably bold step of trusting the people that he had created to tend and care for all of his Creation. Such stewardship is an awesome responsibility, and it is becoming increasingly clear that it is one which we have woefully failed to fulfil.

Voices seeking to deny that a problem exists seem to have become increasingly muted. Yet despite this, and although the World does seem at last to be waking up and recognising the harsh reality, the initiative appears to be slipping away from us, as things seem to go from bad to worse.

It is a telling indictment of the human condition that for all the talk about seriously confronting and tackling climate change issues, we continue with largely unchanged and yet ultimately unsustainable ways of living.

The efforts that we have made so far to tackle the problem continue to look like a case of 'too little, too late'.

Looking at the daily news from around the World, are we still ignoring too many signs suggesting that the chickens really are coming home to roost...?

And yet, despite this gloomy outlook, Christians have a greater hope for fulfilment of Creation. Although for now we can see only glimpses of what is to come, we have God's sure and certain promise that this will come fully to fruition when Jesus returns and the World is restored once more to its perfect state.

Begin

Today, did you notice the colourful sky,
Or the flutter of fallen leaves passing you by?
Did you feel the cool currents that drift on the breeze,
Or watch the birds nesting, secure in the trees?

Did you marvel at patterns, the clouds taking form
As they move from pure white to the dark of the storm?
Did you see the great power as waves crash to shore,
Or the sparkling streams where the water drops pour?

Did you revel as nature began to awake,
The nascent Sun rising to greet the daybreak;
A wonder, the new day about to begin,
With the warmth of the light soft caressing the skin?

The voice of the Maker cannot go unheard,
Gently speaking, such joy in Creation is stirred.
God inhabits it all, with His love unrestrained,
He stands at the peak, where He always has reigned.
If we pause, stop to ponder the works of His hand,
With everything balanced and perfectly planned,
Held by His will alone, all that's made tells the story
Of His goodness and love, of His power and His glory.

For so long God's provision has bountifully bloomed,
But so much that was plenty is being consumed;
The charge to the bottom becoming a race,
As resources are gorged on that we can't replace.
We must look to ourselves, see the part that we play,
For it's been on our watch that it's slipping away.
Now, we stand at the edge and we cannot deny
It could all disappear in the blink of an eye.

So, let's reach for a change, see a paradigm shift
That will prompt us to cherish and nurture God's gift;
To hold fast to its beauty, before it's too late,
Rejecting decline as a permanent state.

The task may be daunting, yet ours to be faced,
For reversing the landslide of ruin and waste.
It has to start somewhere, so let us begin
To engage with the challenge, determined to win.
A different path lies ahead, if we choose it:
But there's no second chance, so let's pray we don't lose it.

Disaster

We've recklessly raced to the rim of disaster,
Unrestrained, running blind, going faster and faster,
Vainly fooling ourselves that we still have control,
And that all that we've broken might yet be made whole.

We're so fixed on the now, we're ignoring tomorrow,
No credit remains to repay what we borrow;
Our actions today bear so little of merit,
For the future we're leaving no one should inherit.

Though above the abyss we now stand on the brink,
Still, it seems we don't see just how low we can sink;
While so focussed on everything we're still accruing,
It's too much to admit all the damage we're doing.

Only tears fill the veil with a handful of longing,
For it's those yet to follow we're fatally wronging;
But we don't seem to care, with no reason for changing,
Our eyes closed to the need for complete rearranging.

Convinced there is time that is still ours to master,
But the wounds we've inflicted need more than a plaster;
And so much wearing thin has been taking its toll,
As if something's gone missing so deep in our soul.

Our appetite seemingly cannot be sated,
As we eat up our World with a greed unabated;
Why can we not see that a storehouse depleted
Will leave every hope for the future defeated?

We're lacking the means to make anything better,
The storms rage so fiercely, we only get wetter;
The cloud covered darkness rolls in to consume us:
Without God's saving grace, it will certainly doom us.

Drown

Some years past we were told that the sky had a hole,
But we didn't stop burning those mountains of coal;
We removed all those trees, planting none in their place,
Left a vast empty gap seen so clearly from space.

We built over land, without thought, unforgiving,
Destroying the natural places for living;
We didn't consider it any concern
When species were lost that would never return.

Though some were suggesting we'd turned up the heat,
That the seas would rise up with the land in retreat,
We thought we could go on the same as before,
A drop in the ocean is all that we saw.

Now we stand at the brink; have we left it too late
To pull the World back from this perilous state?
How long to stand idle, to go with the flow?
If we don't turn the tide, there'll be nowhere to go.

Standing helpless, we watch, with the walls coming down,
Until nothing remains: when the ice melts, we drown.

Boiling Point

The World is clearly burning, but our hearts still run on cold;
We think we've heard it all before, and simply won't be told.
Although the heat is rising, our awareness takes a fall,
Long lost in self-denial, like we haven't heard at all.

We've reached the point of boiling, but the pot is left to simmer,
Too soon found spilling over to a future ever grimmer.
Yet still we're standing idly by, to watch the planet melting;
Our mettle quickly washed away by such unwelcome smelting.

How long before we see the truth: from this there's no returning,
Ignoring everything we've learnt, the World will keep on burning.
The trees that are reduced to ash, the coastlines quickly sinking;
From north to south, poles come apart, and solid ground is shrinking.
The truth that stares us in the face: the clearest of all reasons,
Becoming hard to recognise the lines between the seasons.

In digging down the deepest pit, we add fuel to the fire,
And we too will be fossils if the flames grow any higher.
So now may be our final chance to dampen down the burning:
For once the number's off the scale, there'll be no tide for turning.

Planet

A planet that is dying on its feet
Presents a challenge we are still to meet;
But time is short, no moment to delay,
For this disaster must be turned away.

Though we may find the blame so hard to swallow,
If we don't act, catastrophe may follow;
We have to look beyond the here and now,
To find a different furrow we can plough,
To plant the seed in ways we can sustain,
Instead of turning green to barren plain.

Great movements can begin with smallest voices,
With those who are prepared to face the choices
Between what's tough, and tougher, yet not hide:
Those brave enough to swim against the tide;
Who won't allow regret to be a fetter,
Determined to act now to make things better,
Who recognise the battles to be won,
Rejecting thoughts that nothing can be done.

Our selfish needs this duty must transcend
If we are to reverse the deadly trend;
We must respond to our Creator's call,
For we were made as stewards of it all.
Impassioned, we should be forever driven
To cherish all the wonders God has given.

Beauty Restored

When all was shapeless, without form,
  Delivering order from the storm,
    Of chaos not a single trace:
    The hand of God set all in place.

When all was formless, without shape,
    Out of the darkness the escape
    Was put in motion by His touch,
  From out of nothing made so much;
    He set Creation's power free,
  To form the Earth, the sky, the sea.

And when He spoke, the heavens rang
    As if a billion choirs sang;
    For us composing every note,
    To set the melody afloat,
    Delivering the perfect tune:
  To form the stars, the Sun, the Moon.

  And once the boundaries were set,
  To mark where sea and shoreline met,
And where the sky should have its place
  For day and night to show their face,
  Then came the time, once more, below,
    Creation's juices in full flow:
    He filled the seas, the sky, the land
  With every creature He had planned.

Then, from the dust, the very earth,
From deepest love He gave us birth;
The glory of His work displayed,
To fill the World that He had made;
And, as above it all He stood,
The Lord declared that it was good.

Although this beauty has been marred,
By all our failings deeply scarred,
In His compassion, by His grace,
He makes for us a better place;
For yet a greater world awaits
That's just beyond the city gates,
To where His promise leads us through
When all is changed, remade anew;
For us, a home of boundless worth:
In His new Heaven and new Earth!

Songs of Enlightenment

*For since the creation of the world God's invisible qualities –
his eternal power and divine nature – have been clearly seen,
being understood from what has been made, so that men are
without excuse.*

Romans 1:20

The fool says in his heart, "There is no God."

Psalm 14:1

Big Bang or Big God?

The old chestnut: science or religion; religion or science – but is it really a case of one or the other?

There are many modern scientists and other non-Christian thinkers whose philosophy is firmly set against the existence of God, but who would nevertheless acknowledge the limitations of their knowledge, accepting that – at least for now – there remain things beyond their understanding. Their general expectation, however, would be that, in time, we can rest assured that science will 'fill in the gaps' in what we presently know.

But there have been, and continue to be, many other great scientists and thinkers who take a broader view and whose search for those further answers is made in the context of their faith in Biblical truth.

While scientific investigation and discovery may give us a better understanding of the mechanics of how the World and the wider Universe operates, this will never provide answers to what is arguably the far more important and fundamental questions as to the who: the person who designed and put in place the Created Order (God) and the why: the purpose for which we were made (an eternal existence in a love relationship with God).

These discussions are often muddied by polarised views, in particular about the apparent contradiction between, on the one hand, evolution/natural selection and, on the other, Creation. But contrary to what is commonly suggested, are evolution and belief in a creator God really incompatible?

There is surely no reason in principle to suggest that a supremely powerful creator God could not choose to set Creation in motion through this (or any other) process, should he decide to do so.

Every scientific discovery is simply that – the revelation of another small part of God's Created Order.

There are scientists, and other commentators, who point to the fact that the conditions and circumstances that allowed life to arise on Earth in the first place appear to have been set in the perfect balance for the creation of a sustainable living environment. They also note that the slightest deviation in any of these would have rendered the creation of life impossible.

It seems fanciful, to say the least, to suggest that somehow this just happened and that the Earth 'got lucky'. On the contrary, the fine tuning and complex interwoven balance of everything in Creation make it far more likely that this was no accident or happenstance.

Far from disproving the existence of a creator God, our ever-increasing understanding of a Universe governed by an ordered system of observable rules, points ever more strongly towards there being an ultimate designer, who conceived and put it all together in the first place!

Scientific ideas and theories come and go; new discoveries are constantly disproving and rewriting long-accepted scientific 'truths'.

God, by contrast, is constant and unchanging. For all the supposed intellectual certainties that are asserted by those who put their faith in science alone, they cannot (and never will be able to) provide the answer to the ultimate challenge: for, however, you look at it, the question that we always come back to is this – who made the rules…?

The Rules

"Our minds have proved," the scientists said,
"And all our test results have led
Us to conclude that God is dead.
Science won't be kept at bay,
The 'ancient truths' now swept away,
Enlightenment has won the day."

"And if God was, he was for most
No more than some 'unholy ghost',
Fed by his superstitious host;
A product of the mind instead,
Unreal, he lived in each man's head
To fight against imagined dread."

"In absolutes we place our trust,
Not images that turn to dust,
As, without proof, they surely must.
Our rules and systems stand the test,
By modern knowledge fully blessed,
We have no doubts to be confessed.
We live for now, not for some place
Of which we find no single trace
Within the boundaries of our space."

Consumed by intellectual pride,
The scientists are satisfied,
And real truth is thrown aside.
With confidence they smugly say
They have their proof, they know their way:
To doubt their souls cannot fall prey…

But one thing, still, confounds the fools,
Enthroned on their laboratory stools:
They can't explain who made the rules.

Fooled

The fool who says: 'There is no God',
And will not change their mind,
Cannot complain when, at the end,
They're lost and left behind.

The fool who says: 'I've made the grade',
Content in standing still,
Will find that their inertia
Soon becomes a bitter pill;
In clinging to the ways they've known,
Relying on themselves,
They find the store they shop at
Offers only empty shelves.

The fool who says: 'I have it all',
That 'Life is looking fair',
Will scratch beneath the surface
And discover nothing's there;
That all the things they've gathered,
All their wealth, and pomp and fame,
As dust returns to dust,
So, all of this must go the same.

The fool who says: 'I have my wits,
With everything I know,
Unchallenged, in prosperity,
My life is set to grow',
Cannot complain when, at the end,
As things start to unwind,
When all the lights are going out,
They tumble, flying blind.

The fool who says: 'There's only me,
There's really nothing more;
With all of my achievements,
I've received the highest score',
When called to give a true account
Of everything they've done,
They'll lack what they so sorely need:
Salvation through God's Son.

The fool who claims: 'I know myself,
I always reign supreme,
I've fully earned my place in life,
Fulfilling every dream',
May suffer the illusion
That they're firmly in control:
Yet, gaining the whole World, alas,
They lose their very soul.

Misplaced

It's said you can't rely on faith, on things that you're not seeing,
That it is only flesh and blood that makes a human being.
Dismissing all as fantasy, that trust in God is blind,
Instead, they stake their future on the power of the mind.

They say there is a stance to take from which they won't be moving,
That trust should be confined, applied to what their tests are proving.
The paths they tread with certainty, though called by different name,
Reflect their own self-image and are idols just the same.

Their formulas and theorems on which they place reliance,
They bow down to a different god of reasoning and science.
And yet, their faith is transient, too often fails to last,
As new ideas replace the old consigned to ages past.

Continually seeking, yet unsure of what they'll find,
So many new discoveries that bring a change of mind.
Fixated only on the how, they miss the who and why,
The truth is waiting to be seen, but simply passes by.

It's seen in everything that's made, it couldn't be more clear:
Creation shouts the answers if they just had ears to hear.
If only eyes were opened to the futile means they've chased,
Perhaps, at last, they'd see how far their trust has been misplaced?

Pause

The truth I missed had stared me in the face,
But I, too blind to see, from my sure space,
Convinced of my ability to grow
And cultivate my world, and make it so;
By intellect and reason reassured,
Of everything that I was my own lord.

My observations trusted, ever keen,
Rejecting things I knew could not be seen,
With faith in all the systems known to man,
Convinced that science had the only plan;
Self-satisfied within my safe cocoon:
No thought that maybe I might speak too soon.

Yet, something deep within caused me to think,
I'd overlooked the most important link;
The ball I sought to catch so surely curved:
What came before the start that I observed?

When pondering the limits of my mind
That let so many certainties unwind,
I sensed there must be something more than me,
A vast horizon that I couldn't see:
The things I took for granted since my youth
Were not, perhaps, the arbiters of truth.

You could have seen me as a long-lost cause,
Yet now I know it never made You pause;
You kept on keeping on, no thought to stop,
You persevered when I was fit to drop.
And all those times You found me pushing back,
You still pressed on and never left the track;
There might have been much greater heights to scale,
But You determined I should never fail.

When I stop chasing after empty dreams,
And pausing, let You mend my broken seams:
I only have to open up my heart
For You to bring me to a brand new start.

SONGS OF ETERNITY

...from everlasting to everlasting you are God... a thousand years in your sight are like a day that has just gone by, or like a watch in the night.

Psalm 90:2, 4

A never-ending story

What is eternity? What will it mean to live forever?

Humanly, we exist within strictly time-limited parameters, living with the knowledge that everything has its time and that nothing lasts forever. We are born, we live, we die: end of story; or so many think.

This narrow outlook makes it really difficult for us to get our heads around the possibility of an altogether radically different existence, which is not confined within the closed boundaries of time. And yet, in one form or another, this is what awaits us all.

Unlike us, God exists outside of time and space; he made everything, and he holds the Universe, like a single grain of sand, in his mighty hand. He can see all we are, and all we will ever be, from his unique perspective.

In one sense, it's like the passage of our lives is a film that God is able to run, pause, fast forward or reverse the playback. He observes our yesterdays, our todays, and our tomorrows, in a way that is beyond our understanding or imagination.

One day, this life will end and a new eternity will begin for us. At that point, which of the two forks in the road we find ourselves taking will already have been determined by the choice we make now: whether to

123

accept Jesus' freely offered invitation to follow him into an eternal Heaven, or to decline the offer and look forward instead to the dark and unwelcoming road to everlasting separation from God's goodness.

The wonderful truth is that because of what Jesus has done for us, we can share in an eternity filled with all the good things that God has prepared for us since before the beginning of time; but time is short, and there is an urgent need for us to decide.

One thing is certain: eternity is, by definition, a very long time! How we intend to spend it, and where, and with whom, must surely be one of the most important questions that any of us will ever face.

Today

At six o'clock this morning, the final nail was drawn;
At half past six from top to tail the temple curtain torn.
By seven He'd been taken down and laid behind the stone,
Yet only moments later He'd ascended to His throne.

His power, unleashed, at daybreak, rose in profile with the Sun,
So all who heard would know that restoration had begun.
By noon, the Word had flourished, though full beauty left unfurled,
The faithful still to carry the truth to all the World.

With the day unfolding, though men became estranged,
The Word in all its wonder stayed immutable, unchanged;
A constant in the shifting sand, with people still to choose,
Hour by hour the chance remained to see what they would lose.

Now with the dusk approaching, though shadows whisper doubt,
For those with ears to listen the truth will deafen out.
'Two thousand years, and still no sign', the mockers keen to say,
Yet in God's greater scheme of things, it's barely been a day.

It's only by His mercy that the Sun remains to set,
A final chance for those who haven't made their minds up yet:
So, those who say that if He was, He wouldn't wait this long
To come again, ignore the truth, and couldn't be more wrong.

The Waiting

A sense of great expectancy hung heavy in the air,
The star announcing something new was happening down there;
Presaging a wonder that so long had laid in store:
Good things, in smallest packages, are worth the waiting for.

But thirty years were yet to pass till all was set in motion,
In the eternal scheme of things, a drop into the ocean;
For though the star shone brightly, a new age anticipating,
His rising up was still to come: a king, and yet in waiting.

So long unseen by human eye, yet He is ever here,
Millennia have passed, but still His Spirit draws us near;
We wait in hope, with trust assured in all the Lord has spoken,
Upon the hour that He appoints, the darkness will be broken.

For now, we're living in between time past and yet to come,
Awaiting the last trumpet call, the beating of the drum;
With all remade as it should be, the hour for celebrating:
Restored, completely, to the Lord is surely worth the waiting!

A Grain of Sand

Less than a single grain of sand,
Yet laid secure in Jesus' hand,
I'm safely held, and free from harm,
My soul rests easy, in His palm.
While I'm the smallest of the small
My Saviour will not let me fall,
A precious pearl within a shell;
His living water from the well
Sustaining me, to meet my thirst,
Though I'm the least, He puts me first.

Beyond all reason and all rhyme,
God stands outside our space and time;
And all we are, and all that's made
Continue, while His hand is stayed
In mercy, holding all in place,
Until we meet Him, face to face.

His power truly demonstrated
In every wonder He's created,
Yet all that's seen and everywhere
Is nothing but a breath of air,
A droplet through a tiny pore:
For He is all, and so much more.

Such awesome wonder, that the One
Who made the heavens, Moon and Sun
With just the blinking of an eye,
Stepped down, to live with you and I;
That when this space and time is done,
We'll live in glory with the Son.

SONGS OF HOPE

...we wait eagerly for our adoption as sons, the redemption of our bodies. For in this hope we were saved. But hope that is seen is no hope at all. Who hopes for what he already has? But if we hope for what we do not yet have, we wait for it patiently.

Romans 8:23-25

Trusting the promise

What awaits us after we die and leave our current existence behind? Is there reason to hope for something more, something better, something truly lasting?

The Christian hope is that as a result of Jesus' sacrifice on the Cross, his death and resurrection, God has opened the way for us to be reconciled to him and to live with him in the new eternal Kingdom that will be instituted when Jesus returns.

It is a hope for a life utterly transformed and renewed, as we take our place with Jesus in the new Heaven and the new Earth that will replace the old, when God ultimately will be 'making everything new' (Revelation 21:5).

This is not hope as understood by the World – the uncertain prospect of something that might (or might not) happen – but rather, it is the settled assurance of something that we know, with confidence, will come to pass, albeit in God's perfect timing.

In the meantime, it is a decision to trust in God's promises as set out in Scripture, to wait patiently, and to have an unfailing expectation that those promises will be fulfilled in the passage of time.

Although, from this side of Heaven, it is not ours to know precisely how this all may unfold, we know with certainty from Jesus' own words that putting our trust in him and accepting his free gift of salvation guarantees us a place in the wonderful new Earth and new Heaven to come; a place where we will dwell with and be in a restored relationship with God.

A place:

- to be clothed in new, eternal, imperishable bodies
- to live in perfect harmony with all God's people
- to experience the wonders of a new unspoiled Earth
- to enjoy uninhibited access to and fellowship with God

What's not to like?

A Different Sort of Hope

The hope that we have is a different sort,
It cannot be earned and it cannot be bought;
It's a hope that is grown with God's love at the core,
Trusting in Him, we will need nothing more.

The hope that is ours of a different ilk:
For us, as His children, our life-giving milk;
A hope that provides us the richest of fare,
Through faith that is nourished by God's loving care.

The hope we once had in ourselves overpriced,
When the One we should seek is our Lord Jesus Christ;
The things of this World in which we choose to trust,
So soon disappeared and consigned to the dust.

The hope that we have is in a different class,
It's not just a sense of what may come to pass:
It's a deeper conviction of what is to be,
An undeserved future, that's offered for free,
Which, should we accept, through the promise He's making,
Is written, assured, and is ours for the taking.

The price has been paid, we can know beyond doubt,
The Lord is our Saviour at life's final shout;
His certain redemption of all of our sin,
The hope of the ages will gather us in.

Our hope's not just a vague anticipation,
But, fuelled by faith, on fire with expectation.

New

When our time on this Earth is done,
When we are called to meet God's Son,
How different will our living be,
When from the dark He sets us free?

There'll be new Heaven and new Earth,
A life of everlasting worth,
Of endless peace, and love and joy,
Where rust and moth cannot destroy;
Where longing hearts at last are stilled,
Our souls by Him completely filled.

There'll be no Sun, no night and day,
His face will shine an endless ray;
For He alone our one true light,
A love that's making all things right.

The river pouring down the street,
Where Jesus' power and beauty meet,
The waters fresh, untainted, pure,
From every ill, the perfect cure;
A place unlike the World we've known,
Now only goodness will be grown:
New life that blooms in fertile soil,
A harvest reaped without the toil.

There'll be no longing, no regret,
With all our needs completely met;
In every way we'll be fulfilled,
All things made new, as He has willed;
His praise will be our one desire,
To sing His name and lift Him higher.

In this new city we'll be found,
With those in faith who held their ground;
A place beyond our wildest dreams,
With wonders bursting at the seams;
His people gathered, all as one,
To reign forever with the Son.

It surely will be just like this:
A place of peace, eternal bliss;
When with the saints we take our place,
At last, we'll see Him, face to face,
Safe in new Heaven and new Earth:
We'll know true life in all its worth.

Not Falling Apart

We don't have to see everything falling apart;
If our will has been broken; and, contrite in heart,
We face up to adversity coming our way,
In the knowledge that God has the ultimate say.

There's no obstacle ever too high to be scaled
When we think of the hands and the feet that were nailed;
By surrendering all to the Father's good will,
We will find there is no insurmountable hill.

When we take it to heart, when we know death is done,
We can put all our hope in the love of the Son;
When the Lord comes again, and releases our chains,
Then there'll be nothing left but discarded remains
Of the burdens that held us for such a short time,
When compared to the eternal life, so sublime.

There is nothing of worth that is falling apart;
When God turns it around, then true living can start.

Storms

To the trials of life, faith should not make us blind,
When we walk through the fire, our souls are refined;
When we trust God's provision, it's then that we learn,
Though flames may surround us, He won't let us burn.

We won't walk on water, our feet will get wet,
For the challenges faced are not done with us yet;
It will not be plain sailing, the wind has to turn,
The oceans will rise and the sea will still churn.

He won't block out the static, or smother the noise,
When rancour abounds and the silence destroys;
Yet just when the weight of the World takes its toll,
His still quiet voice is a balm to the soul.

He will lift on broad shoulders when waters are deep,
He will be the sure rope when the climb is too steep;
He will cling to us tightly, He'll not let us fall,
When we trust in His name, He will answer our call.

He won't calm every gale, pacify every wave,
But He hears our appeal when we ask Him to save;
He will walk alongside us at every turn,
Assuaging our doubts, meeting every concern;
He will share every burden and carry our pain,
He's with us today, and He'll always remain.

We can ride out the storms with our confidence high,
With Him on our side, we can never say die;
Our future secure, He is ever our friend,
The outcome assured, we are His to the end.

Starting Over

It is not all over; it's about to begin:
No longer held down by the burden of sin,
The limits and chains of the temporal perished,
He's standing, remade, in a place to be cherished.

For those left behind, there's a sadness in parting,
Yet the life he was made for is only just starting;
Something new and amazing for him has begun,
Holding fast to the victory that Jesus has won;
And there's comfort in knowing, as God's Word is spoken,
That He is restoring what once was so broken.

We recall, when we think our resolve may be cracked,
This is only the interval, not the last act;
For the set is transformed on the turn of a page:
Now he's treading the boards of a different stage.

Although grief's deeply felt, it can't hold us too long,
When we know he has joined in a beautiful song,
And has taken his place in God's Heavenly choir,
With a chorus of angels, his voice lifted higher.

Alive with the Father, assurance eternal,
A glory that grows from the tiniest kernel;
Becoming the fullness that God had intended:
Past hurts put aside, now so totally mended.

It isn't the end, it's a glorious beginning:
No losers in Heaven, God's love ever winning;
When, like him, we're called home, having finished the race,
We will all meet again, in that wonderful place.

SONGS OF INVITATION

[Jesus said] "Ask and it will be given to you; seek and you will find; knock and the door will be opened to you…"

Matthew 7:7

[Jesus said] "Here I am! I stand at the door and knock. If anyone hears my voice and opens the door, I will come in and eat with him, and he with me."

Revelation 3:20

RSVP

What informs our response when we receive an invitation to a celebration, or to some other event? How well we know the host? Whether there will be like-minded people with whom we will enjoy spending time? The location and the ambience of the venue? Or, perhaps, we have something else that we would prefer to be doing at that time.

Whatever our thoughts, the choice to accept or decline is ours and ours alone.

In the same way, Jesus' offer of salvation and new life is made by way of an invitation, which leaves the response wholly in our hands.

The Lord of all Creation calls us to join with him in the joy and exultation of a wonderful eternal celebration. But at the end of the day, it is we who have the freedom to choose: to accept or to decline. There is no half-way house, there can be no hedging our bets; ignoring the invitation, or failing to respond is as good as saying no.

Can we afford to pass up such an amazing opportunity, forgoing our place in the everlasting Heavenly community of God and his people? Do we really have somewhere better to be?

And surely, we should be doing all that we can to ensure that everyone knows that this glorious invitation is open to them too, so that they don't miss out?

Beside the Road

I saw a man, stood tall beside the road,
He said that He would bear my every load;
That all my burdens would be His to hold,
If I should choose to come in from the cold;
That I could walk the road without the weight,
To find myself a wholly different state;
Relieved of what had held me down before,
Discovering what wonders lay in store.

Though there was so much more to gain than lose,
He told me it was wholly mine to choose,
And graciously left me the final say,
The freedom, still, to go another way,
Not reaching out to take His offered hand,
Determined, in my pride, alone to stand.

The chance, if not embraced, would soon be gone,
If I should stand, refusing to move on;
Instead, by running scared the other way,
To every doubt my soul still falling prey,
I clung to the familiar that had failed
To lead me out of darkness that assailed,
I surely would be lost and left behind,
The road to bring me home not mine to find.

If only I would stop, and take it in,
The promise of a different way begin,
Allowing my thin cover to be blown,
Accepting greater guidance than my own,
Then even through the trouble and the strife,
I'd chart a course that offered me true life:
My highway subject to a different code,
With Jesus walking with me on the road.

Open Door

When you have been outside so long, no thought of coming in,
Stood all alone, it seems so hard to know where to begin.
It's like finding a door ajar that's been slammed in your face,
With any hope of passing through long vanished, without trace.

It's like the key has fallen out, the door left firmly locked,
Your passage to the other side forever wholly blocked.
It's like the door's been boarded up, the nails so firmly driven;
That this can never be undone, no second chances given.

Yet through the darkness, seeping through, the glimmer of a candle;
And if you take another look, you just might see the handle
Is really there in front of you, set ready for the turning;
While, waiting on the other side, a brighter light is burning.
The simple truth discovered: it isn't you outside,
But Jesus who is longing for your door to be flung wide;
He wants to come to heal your heart, the change anticipating,
But leaves the choice within your hands, in love and mercy, waiting.

A heart accepting Jesus' grace, He'll never be refusing;
So, you can be an open door: the time is yours, for choosing.

Discontented

I dreamt of what was still to come, when to His House God takes me,
A matchless celebration, when in love the Lord remakes me.

The party was a strange affair, for others should have been there;
What could have led them somewhere else, to stop them being seen
there?
I felt a sense of discontent and couldn't seem to shake it:
That though I had been Heaven-sent, those others didn't make it.

Just for a moment, so confused, I couldn't understand it:
For surely this could not have been the way that God had planned it?
Why had so many turned Him down, His open invitation;
Stood on the platform when the train had long gone from the station?

But then, a revelation struck: what story did I sell them?
Or had I simply passed them by, and just forgot to tell them?
How many seeds were left unsown, how many words unspoken,
My token efforts to repair that left them lost and broken?

I dreamt that, still with time to come, I'd seek the missing numbers;
That God might stir my empty heart, to rouse me from my slumbers.
So, when, at last, He calls me home, my hope to be excited:
To join the celebration, with so many more invited!

Come to Him

Come to Him,
When you are feeling beaten, so downtrodden and forlorn,
As if the pages of your life have been forever torn.
When all the keys you held that once appeared to set things right,
No longer fit, and every door, it seems, is now shut tight;
When you have run so low, and now the tank has been left dry:
Familiar fumes long faded that no longer get you high;
When you are lost, and find that true direction's hard to find,
The darkness ever closing in that leaves you flying blind.

Come,
When you are feeling there's no more that you can do:
When all you have is emptiness and failure seeping through;
When it is all for nothing that it seems you vainly wait,
For scant relief that's never found, the foe stood at the gate;
When all the powers of the World weigh heavy, looming large,
And having the last word, it seems they'll always be in charge.

Come,
When hope in all the World may give has worn so thin,
And what you seek, instead, is for a new life to begin;
There's nothing that you have to pay, admission's offered free:
Jesus longs to welcome you, to where you're meant to be;
Straight into the final round, already qualified:
It's yours to share the victory, as you join the winning side.

So, come to Heaven's certainty, no more to roll the dice,
Secure in knowing all is done, our Lord has paid the price;
You'll find that there's a place reserved already with your name:
For you have been expected, you were known before you came.
The voices of the World that shout so loud are all struck dumb,
Drowned by the Lord's sweet calling as He bids us, simply, come.

SONGS OF PURPOSE

We have this hope as an anchor for the soul, firm and secure.

Hebrews 6:19

Since, then, you have been raised with Christ, set your hearts on things above, where Christ is seated at the right hand of God. Set your minds on things above, not on earthly things… you have taken off your old self…and have put on the new self, which is being renewed in knowledge in the image of its Creator…

Colossians 3:1-2, 9-10

New age or new life?

God is no more the product of the Twenty-First Century than he is the product of the First Century. He is who he is: unchanging, the same now and always.

An attitude that appears to be gaining ever increasing traction today is the assertion that 'it doesn't matter what I believe, so long as it works for me'.

We find ourselves in an increasingly self-reliant society, with the individual at the centre, where what 'I' enjoy, or want, or believe, is all that really counts. No surprise, then, that there is a common tendency to mould beliefs around existing lifestyles, rather than the other way around.

Any challenge to our attitudes, behaviour and beliefs can simply be headed off by taking a 'pick and mix' approach to religion and belief systems: a bit of this belief, a pinch from another, some part of a third and so on, until we have what fits together comfortably and consistently with the position that we have chosen to adopt.

The sad truth, however, is that all that this is likely to produce is a shallow, diluted and meaningless froth.

Why is Christianity failing to engage with so many people today?

If there is a Biblical view that makes us feel uncomfortable, if it calls into question aspects of our lives or patterns of behaviour that we would rather not be brought to light, the easy solution is to reject that element as outmoded, or out of touch with our modern 'enlightened' way of thinking.

Coupled with this, we also see misguided attempts to reinterpret fundamental truths, reinventing the Jesus of the Bible to fit in with our ever-changing morals and attitudes, in an effort to transform what looks like a dusty set of ancient and outdated views into something more 'fit for purpose' in the modern world.

Such an attempt to make Christianity more attractive and acceptable to an increasingly secular society, seeking to embrace the shifting sands of the World's standards, while pushing to one side those aspects of faith which sit awkwardly with worldly views of right and wrong, is ultimately futile and doomed to failure.

Integrity still counts.

People will not be so easily fooled: for all such efforts to 'modernise' expressions of faith, they are not flocking back into the arms of the Church. A belief system that alters or discards, with the seasons, its most basic and underlying moral foundations, will soon be found out and will come to be seen as nothing more than an empty and hollow shell of its true self, with nothing to offer a world searching for answers to life's fundamental questions.

But at the end of the day, it is really not about churches, or buildings, or organisations: the key is our personal relationship with the One who made us and loves us beyond measure. He is the God of Heaven, but he is also as close to us as a father and a brother.

What are we really looking for? How are we to find a truth that endures?

We each have a choice: to spend our lives wandering aimlessly along the cratered road of our ever-changing preferences, or to anchor ourselves instead in the safe haven of the unchanging Creator and sustainer of everything.

Is it really such a hard choice to make?

Roads

In this enlightening new age of individual choice,
Old certainties are washed away where truth has lost its voice;
Just like the cat that gets the cream, contentedly they purr,
A melting pot of strange ideas, but nothing makes them stir.

They speak as if the Galilean, though a man of worth,
Was not come down from Heaven, but was wholly of the Earth;
"This idea of exclusiveness", they say, "is really odd",
"If all roads lead to Rome, then surely all must lead to god".

So, finding god in all, and all in god, as one, the same,
The difference insubstantial, when it's only in the name;
They stay content, to pick and mix, but just the sweetest parts –
No bitter truths admitted that might sour complacent hearts.

They speak as if they're self-made men, enthralled by their own powers:
"If we're made in god's image, then he's surely made in ours".
And even midst the ranks of those who lead, who claim to know,
To fit their lifestyles, make, instead, a dozen ways to go.

So, from their self-sufficiency they will not go astray,
Ignoring, in their vanity, the signs that point the way -
The Cross awaits, to free us all, to walk the path He trod:
All roads lead to Rome, but only one road leads to God.

Follow the Star

If we open our hearts to a different view,
There's a light that will lead us to something so true.
As we're drawn to go further and travelling far,
Like the Magi, determined to follow the star.

It burns like a fire, with love at its source,
Bright shining the way to a different course.
To step into the light, or to hide in the shade:
To follow the star is a choice to be made.

Freedom is offered from shackles that bind,
As the burdens that hold us begin to unwind.
If we push at the door, He will open it wide,
When we follow the star, we'll be welcomed inside.

Not by our endeavours, it's given for free,
It's for us to embrace, if we have eyes to see.
The decision is ours at the end of the day:
We can follow the star, or just go on our way.

Still illuming Creation, the darkness recedes,
He will show us the path and will meet all our needs.
No bag and no purse, if we come as we are,
His provision is sure, when we follow the star.

So we bring what we can, letting Him do the rest,
For it's only by grace that we truly are blessed.
His power to heal can remove every scar,
Our living transformed when we follow the star.

There's a strange revolution, our longing complete,
When we scatter our crowns as we fall at His feet.
With a call to be humble, discarding all pride,
It's our hearts that He wants, setting all else aside.

There is no better time to be seeking the King,
For to walk in His light is to change everything.
The journey's worth making, no matter how far;
True wisdom is ours, when we follow the star.

More Than Me

There was a time when I believed my star shone like the Sun,
That round my very centre every orbit had to run;
Assured of everything I had, a fixed and settled core,
The source of my own light and heat, I needed nothing more;
Imagining I was the lord of all that I could see:
I never stopped to think there may be something more than me.

Convinced that everything I grew would meet my every need,
All of my own creation, having planted every seed,
It seemed my self-sufficiency would stand me in good stead,
That every grain produced would satisfy, with daily bread.

I clung to the illusion this was all of my own making,
Rooted firmly in my ground, and not a tree for shaking,
My branches stretching proudly to an ever-brightening sky:
I never entertained the thought of something more than I.

So wrapped up in my own small thoughts of how I ought to live,
I didn't see how little that was truly mine to give,
How fragile and how fickle and how quickly washed away,
So surely gone tomorrow, even though it's here today.

Consumed by my own sense of worth, inflated, overblown:
I'd not conceived of power that was greater than my own.
This sober revelation, still I failed to realise
That all that seemed so certain could unwind before my eyes;
Still straining every sinew to the very nth degree,
I never had the sense there might be something more than me.

Although, through every challenge, I'd not let myself be phased,
Still thinking that my industry was something to be praised,
A simple realisation would in time be mine to learn:
My empty self-importance was a vanity to spurn.
I'd not foreseen a victory, except the one I owned,
Yet down from my high pedestal too soon to be dethroned.

For setting my agenda as if I was in control,
Selecting the direction towards which I sought to roll,
Was nothing but delusion, all my mettle turned to rust,
If all that I had thought secure was trampled in the dust.

My momentary bubble was surely set to burst,
Last place would be my ending by my always seeking first;
There had to be another way, to set my spirit free:
If only I acknowledged there was something more than me.

The dawning of a different day saw my perspective shift:
That all I had was given by the Lord, a precious gift;
In Him my every purpose met, the King of all my days,
I could not help but turn to God and give Him all my praise.

His Spirit moved within me, with my deepest longing stirred,
My heart and soul enraptured by the beauty of His Word,
An end to all my striving that could never satisfy,
Eyes opened to His promise and my every reason why;
Turned out instead of inward, scales had fallen, let me see:
The wondrous truth that there is something so much more than me!

Sufficient

The little that I bring for You may be the very least,
Yet still You load my table with the greatest kind of feast;
And in my insufficiency, my weakness fully shown:
When all my trust is placed in You, is when my faith is grown.
Though scraps are all I have to give, my offerings so poor,
You multiply my little into something so much more;
My efforts, though they seem in vain, with little progress seen,
You take my small, and make complete, and fill the gaps between.

The all I have is not enough to face down darker powers,
For none of us alone can win: the battle isn't ours.
My faith in You, your love for me, together will unite us,
By trust, I'll see your cause prevail, defeating those who fight us.
Although the World can't understand, my weakness makes me stronger,
It's when I pull the shortest straw, and can't go on much longer,
I understand that all You ask: to give my best in trying,
My knowing that it's You alone on whom I am relying.

You can take a dying breath and make it come alive:
If You can feed five thousand with a meal that's made for five,
Then anything is possible, with You as the Creator;
Although my all is meagre, in your hands it's so much greater.
The little that is mine to give may be the very least,
But when I trust in You alone, when foolish pride is ceased,
I live to bring You glory when your plans through me succeed,
Surrendering to your good will: your grace is all I need.

SONGS OF THE KINGDOM COME

...Jesus went into Galilee, proclaiming the good news of God. "The time has come," he said. "The kingdom of God is near. Repent and believe the good news!"

Mark 1:14-15

Breaking through

We live in between times.

Although through the life, death and resurrection of Jesus, God's Kingdom has in a very tangible sense 'broken into' the World in which we live, the process remains incomplete.

And until Jesus returns to restore the World to the perfect state that he originally intended, we can only experience a fraction of the wonders that await us in Heaven.

It sometimes feels as if we have one foot in the doorway to Heaven, but the other still firmly and frustratingly stuck in the here and now.

In those moments, when we long to escape the ravages of this fractious World in which we find ourselves, we can take comfort from the promise of what is yet to come, as so wonderfully revealed in God's Word.

We can rest secure in knowing that by putting our trust in Jesus, we have a glorious homecoming waiting for us in the Kingdom to come!

King

What kind of king, stepping down from His throne,
In the greatest expression of love ever known,
So much more than the princes of Earth have to give,
Lays His majesty down, so that others might live?

What kind of king, putting stars into space,
The Creator of every creature and place,
Departing the wonders of Heavenly light,
Comes to give life, to bring day out of night?

What kind of king, setting powers aside,
Shows a strength born through weakness that can't be denied?
Becomes one of us in such frailty and pain,
Giving all of Himself, for our personal gain?

What kind of king is He, bearing no sword,
Whose faithfulness brings an eternal reward?
No matter the cost, it's a price He will meet,
Consigning the darkness to certain defeat.

What kind of king? He's the greatest of all:
We are held in His hand, He will never let fall;
By His grace we are saved, as He makes us His own,
Truly blessed, let us worship at His glorious throne!

Heaven's Doorway

Standing on the threshold, but my time has not yet come
To hear the closing chords, the final beating of the drum;
The door, ajar, is beckoning to something fresh and new:
One foot in Heaven's doorway, but the other still not through.

Standing on the threshold, I'm awaiting the full flow
Of waters to transform anew, but time is running slow;
The hour, still, is yet to come, the tide far from the beach:
One foot in Heaven's doorway, but the other out of reach.

Standing on the threshold, I just want to take a look
At all that waits for me inside, the promise of the Book;
The hour, though, is still far off, a light seen through a crack:
One foot in Heaven's doorway, but the other still held back.

Standing on the threshold, with my patience wearing thin,
Longing for the time to come when I'll be welcomed in;
The hour, though, is not yet here for all to open wide:
One foot in Heaven's doorway, but the other still outside.

Standing on the threshold of a Kingdom come in part,
Although not fully here for now, still warms my thankful heart;
The hour God's alone to choose – what joy will then be found:
To enter Heaven's doorway, with both feet on holy ground!

Yet

When times feel such a burden, weighing heavy on your soul,
Remember God's beside you, He is always in control.
When you are tempted to indulge self-pity and regret,
Remember God's still working: He's not finished with you yet.

And when you find the pain too much, held captive by such loss,
Remember Jesus bore a greater measure on the Cross.
The road you walk's a journey; when you find the going tough,
Remember your God understands, He's with you through the rough.

When all the World's against you or, at least, that's how it seems,
Remember God is faithful and His sacrifice redeems.
When everything seems just too hard, fit only to forget,
Remember God's still with you: He's not finished with you yet.

Time

It's time for us to slow it down;
Though wanting to go faster,
We cannot let the pressing day
Become our lord and master.

We need some moments to reflect,
Select a lower gearing;
Apply a more discerning ear,
To take in what we're hearing.

In giving ourselves time to breathe,
A pace more ably bearing,
We'll surely better understand
What God is truly sharing.

Such priceless gift, so dearly made,
Should not be treated cheaply,
We have to let each precious word
Speak to our hearts more deeply.

For when we let the essence flow
Like rivers, running through us,
He'll lead us to absorb the depths
Of love He's bringing to us.

To be the best part of each day
Should be our constant seeking;
There's nothing more to set the tone
Than hearing Jesus speaking.

The Word of God is life itself,
It's freely given for us:
If we surrender to His voice,
In time, He will restore us.

Old Made New

If the Old was good, then the New is better;
In Him, I hang on every letter,
The Word of God, through Jesus spoken,
The Old made New is never broken:
A covenant of love and grace
That time and tide cannot replace.

The endless bounty of the Lord
So great, though I could not afford,
He gave Himself, His all my gain,
To set me free from every chain.

The place that I inhabit now,
Eternity does not allow;
I seek the city yet to come,
The rhythm of a different drum.

What can mere mortals do to me,
When God's already set me free?
The lure of worldly things grows dim,
I look for nothing else but Him.

So, this should be my sacrifice:
To give my all and not think twice,
Responding to my Saviour's call,
In doing good and sharing all.
I pray to keep my loving true,
To honour Him in all I do:
Above all else, to give Him praise,
My songs of joy through endless days!

Songs of Worth

You were taught, with regard to your former way of life, to put off your old self…; to be made new in the attitude of your minds; and to put on the new self, created to be like God in true righteousness and holiness.

Ephesians 4:22-24

Known by God

How are we to find our place in the World?

There may be times or circumstances that make us wonder just how we fit as individuals into our complex and often confusing World. For some, this can develop into a real struggle to find a sense of true personal worth.

The anchor to which we choose to secure ourselves will largely determine the person that we let ourselves become; it is a choice that we should not make lightly.

The modern world bombards us with a muddled array of competing ideas: how can we see through this fog of confusion?

From a Christian viewpoint, it seems only natural that we should align ourselves with someone who knows us better than we know ourselves.

Who better than our Creator to affirm who we are made to be?

Someone Else's Son

When I was someone else's son
I couldn't find the door,
I held the key within my hand,
But didn't know what for.
It was as if I sang the words
To someone else's songs,
A lost, estranged, relation,
So unsure where he belongs.
It felt like any moment
Everything would come undone:
I wasn't where I should have been,
As someone else's son.

When I was someone else's son,
I didn't realise
That He'd already made me His,
It came as some surprise.
He didn't wait for me to change,
Because my love He yearned,
Embraced me as His very own,
Despite the grace I spurned.
Back then, I hadn't recognised
That He must be the One,
Caught up in my confusion,
Being someone else's son.

When I was someone else's son,
Unseen, what good things were,
The riches that could fill my soul
Lay dormant, yet to stir.
But God was so determined,
There was nowhere I could hide,
His plans could not be shaken off,
No matter how I tried.
He called my name, He sought me out,
To come in from the cold,
Restored to Heaven's family,
Drawn back within the fold.

So happy to be home at last,
There is no better place
To find my true allegiance,
Than secured by Jesus' grace.
In Him, my true identity:
By Him, I'm fully known;
No longer someone else's son,
But His, and His alone.

Called by Name

When God first spoke my name, I wasn't listening,
I didn't hear Him calling me by name;
I didn't know that this was my true christening,
That it was Him, alone, designed my frame.

When God first spoke my name, I wasn't waiting
For any help, I did it on my own,
Without a sense of hope, anticipating
A future, self-absorbed and so alone.

When God first spoke my name, I was distracted,
I didn't hear the sweetness in His voice;
Unhearing and unmoved, I'd not reacted,
So unaware He offered me a choice.

When God first spoke my name, I wasn't hearing;
I didn't know he hung on every word,
My silence turned to mocking and to jeering,
That left His call to me, ignored, unheard.

When God first spoke my name, I wasn't praying,
I had no sense of all that it involved;
Still, all the foolish plans that I'd been laying
Left my eternal future unresolved.

So, when He calls your name, though no one's speaking,
For once, step out, surrender your control,
Accept the peace you hadn't thought of seeking,
Give Him the space to touch your very soul.
For once you know that voice, embrace the hearing,
The darkness disappears without a trace;
Give Him all your anxiety and fearing,
Dwell long within the wonders of His grace.

When God first spoke my name, I wasn't listening:
But now I hear Him calling me by name.

What It's All About

When we set ourselves up as the lords of our fate,
Will we see danger coming before it's too late?
Will there be only rocks onto which we are driven?
What is it all for, this short time that we're given?

It's about leaving more than we had when we started,
It's about seeking goodness, to be open-hearted;
It's about being generous throughout changing seasons,
And being remembered for all the right reasons.

It's about making others the heart of our being,
And opening our eyes to the things that they're seeing;
It's about going last when we could have been first,
It's about being ready to quench others' thirst.

It's about being humble, not chasing the proud,
Content not to be standing out in the crowd;
It's not about self, not to be number one,
But praising the good in what others have done.

It's about trust in God, when our own strength is failing,
Assured that His enduring love is prevailing;
And never surrendering to frailties and fears,
Letting His gentle hand wipe away all our tears.
It's about being thankful for all that He's giving,
Embracing with joy His good purpose for living,
When every concern becomes faded and dim:
For it's not about us: it is all about Him!

SONGS FOR A TIME YET TO COME

PART 3: THE COMPASSIONATE GOD

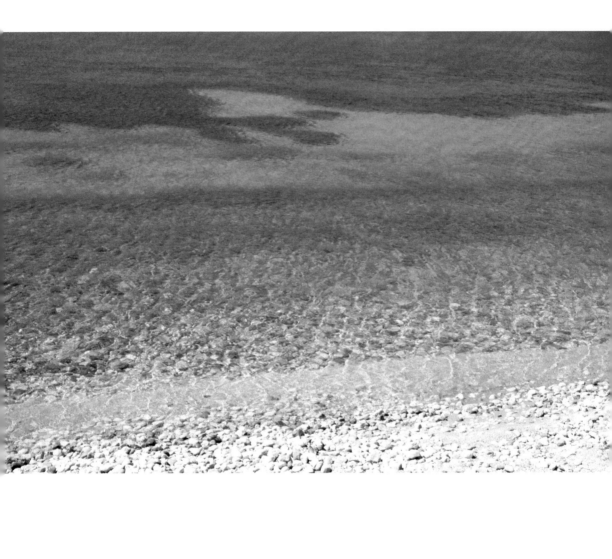

SONGS OF COMFORT

Praise be to the God and Father of our Lord Jesus Christ, the Father of compassion and the God of all comfort, who comforts us in all our troubles, so that we can comfort those in any trouble with the comfort we ourselves have received from God.

2 Corinthians 1:3-4

In times of trouble

No matter what life may throw at us, we have the reassurance that Jesus is always there to walk beside us and to comfort us, even in our darkest hour and even when we are at our lowest ebb.

He lived as a human being, like you and me. He knows what it is like to face ridicule, rejection, betrayal, hatred, abandonment, isolation and ultimately a cruel death. No one could empathise more with our trials and tribulations; and no one has the power that he possesses to meet every challenging situation head-on and to change our situation for the better.

Being a follower of Jesus will not insulate us from troubles, from difficulties, from failures or even disasters, but we can be sure that through it all he will be there as our supporter and comforter.

And, with the assurance of his comfort for us, we in turn are enabled to share that comfort with others, to help them through their own difficult times.

179

Knowing

The Lord stepped down from glory for our sake,
A life as one of us He chose to make.
And being here among us, as a man,
He put in motion God's salvation plan.

He felt the joys that love and friendship bring,
Was even hailed, but briefly, as the King.
He hoped for much, yet saw things going wrong,
He mourned for loss and joined the plaintive song.

He tasted triumph, suffered greater loss,
Was cast aside and cruelly cut across.
He knew the ups and downs that we all face,
Was lifted high, then mired in our disgrace.
He was cast down, to deepest depths was thrown,
Ignored, rejected, utterly alone.

He knows about our struggles, how we've tried,
He'll be the source of comfort, walk beside,
To strengthen us in all we're going through,
When others turn away, He will be true.
There's nothing we can say He hasn't heard,
We can be sure His love for us is stirred;
He feels our very longings as His own,
He'll honour every prayer, each silent groan.

So, when we lay our heart within His hands,
We can be sure that Jesus understands
Our anger, our frustration, all our pain,
That make His tears pour down like autumn rain.

He joins us in the darkness that we face,
He's freely chosen dying in our place,
A precious gift that we could not afford,
An endless grace that's given by the Lord.

We come to Him in confidence complete,
To lay our every burden at His feet;
He's been for us before the World began:
Our Saviour, fully God, yet fully man!

Never Alone

In moments when you think that no one else can feel your pain,
When calling into emptiness appears a lone refrain,
There's someone who will hear your every sigh, each silent moan,
To offer true assurance: you don't need to be alone.

He will be always there for you, from first until the last,
Your solitary confinement will be banished to the past.
Though now may seem the darkest night that you have ever known,
When Jesus walks beside you, you will not be left alone.

When hopelessness confronts you and it threatens to consume,
That's when the hope that He provides will come into full bloom;
If you stay rooted in Him, though the fiercest wind has blown,
He'll be your firm foundation, when you trust in Him alone.

So, if you share it all with Him, however great your grief,
He'll bring a peace into your heart, the sweetest of relief;
For when you walk beside Him, as you see your faith full grown,
Then, even in your darkest night, you'll never be alone.

Upside Down

There are times when it all comes apart at the seams,
When it's like being plagued by the strangest of dreams,
When nothing makes sense, the World looks upside down,
And it feels like my face wears a permanent frown

As I pick through the bones of what's left of the day,
It just seems there is nothing that's going my way;
Through a fog of confusion, hemmed in all around,
Everything I once knew has been going to ground.
The flowers reduced to the weakest of shoots,
In a tangle of wood where I trip on the roots,
Where the colour fades out to the palest of hues,
As my feelings descend to the deepest of blues.

I just can't shake it off, that there's something so wrong,
Like the singer has mixed up the words of the song,
With the music discordant, off pitch, not in key,
All the notes out of place and not where they should be.
When it seems that there's simply nowhere left to turn,
That I no longer have any bridges to burn,
That I'm just hanging on by the flimsiest cord:
Only then do I look to the grace of the Lord.

And I wonder why this has been so long delayed,
How much easier it would have been if I'd just prayed,
And sought my security from the one place
That ensures I'm protected by unending grace.

When it seems that I simply have no more to give,
He provides everything that I need just to live
In a way from the start that He always intended,
With every bridge that I've burnt fully mended,
Everything that I've damaged, now fully restored,
Through the unending power and grace of the Lord.
From the doubts that before all around had assailed me,
As all my vain efforts fell short and just failed me,
He replaces my loss with the greatest of winnings,
Turning everything round from the least of beginnings.

From all of my failures so freely forgiving,
He's leading me home to a new way of living;
And I wonder, again, how I'd not seen before
All the wonder that following Him has in store.
Now, at last, right side up, with my balance resetting,
The salvation He brings I cannot be forgetting;
For it's only in Him that it's all making sense,
With the Lord as my present, and my future tense.

Coming Up for Air

When in the face of tragedy, God brings His gentle healing,
It feels like standing up once more, after so long kneeling.

It feels like someone takes our hand, after so long lonely,
With reconnection being made, no longer one and only.

It feels like coming into sight, after so long hidden,
The darkness that long weighed us down, at last is overridden.

It feels like finding a new tune, after so long singing
Discordant, unfamiliar tones, that in our ears were ringing.

It feels like storm has eased to calm, after so long churning,
Head now held above the waves, the tide, it seems, is turning.

When we might ever breathe again, we had begun to wonder:
It feels like coming up for air, after so long under.

Though life may bring its tragedies, they can't forever hold us,
For we can find true comfort when we let God's love enfold us.

Not Wearing Black

With so much darkness swirling all around,
When hope is not so easy to be found,
When we sense our resolve begin to crack:
The time, it seems, is ripe for wearing black.

For now, obscured, the light is heavy veiled,
With thoughts of loss our senses are assailed,
When we are so far off the beaten track,
We join the line of mourners, wearing black.

From so much sadness finding no relief,
Too soon deep buried in a mound of grief,
Retreating from the enemy's attack,
There's nothing left for us but wearing black.

Yet there remains a different path to tread,
Where God will shine the light of hope instead,
Restoring loss and everything we lack:
That speaks of something more than wearing black.
The Lord assures us that the ones we've missed,
Who by His resurrection power are kissed,
With Him, one day, will soon be coming back,
And there will be no cause for wearing black.

When we remember everything He's done,
The power of death defeated by His Son;
When we recall the promises He's made,
That we will join His victory parade;
When we accept that He is in control,
And holds the fate of every faithful soul,
With confidence, we take a different tack:
Our mourning passed, no longer wearing black.

We do not face an ending without hope,
He gives us all we need, and more, to cope,
To bear a sadness that will not endure,
For His salvation power is the cure.
Our God will always put us back on track:
Clothed in His robes of white, instead of black.

SONGS OF COMMITMENT

Then Jesus said to his disciples, "If anyone would come after me, he must deny himself and take up his cross and follow me. For whoever wants to save his life will lose it, but whoever loses his life for me will find it."

Matthew 16:24-25

No matter the cost

No one can earn their way to Heaven; there is nothing that we can do ourselves to receive salvation. It is entirely due to God's love for us that we can be saved; and it is a gift that is offered for free. But we have to make the choice to accept what God offers us.

Our natural response to such a gift should be to instill in us a desire and a determination to live our lives in the way that God would have us live.

When life throws challenges at us that appear to be insurmountable, and when our instinct is to keep our heads down and just play things safe, we must never lose sight of the fact that Jesus paid the ultimate price in giving up his very life so that we could live.

In a world obsessed with self-fulfilment, where personal happiness takes centre-stage, it is too easy to overlook the many individual examples of sacrificial giving and commitment to the needs and wellbeing of others all around us – if we only have eyes to see.

As followers of Jesus, Christians are called to put their faith on the line, to make a real commitment to follow him, no matter what the personal cost may be. Each new day brings opportunities to make this a reality.

This goes far beyond a mere acknowledgement of all the good things that he gives us, important as that is. It calls for a settled determination on our part never to waver in trusting him, through thick and thin; it means sticking with him just the same, both in good times and bad.

Although we can never hope to match his absolute commitment to us, we can nevertheless choose to press in to him as far as we are able and, in doing so, make a real difference in our lives and in the lives of those with whom we come into contact.

No Longer Hiding

Today must see the hour of our starting:
We must be ready for a sure departing;
To heal the hurt across our fractured nation,
We can't remain, unmoving, in the station.

Today must be the time for us, deciding
To move into the light, no longer hiding;
As all our weaknesses, truly confessing,
Are turned by Him into a holy blessing
For those He'd have us reach with His compassion,
Prepared to give our all, our every ration.

We have to be the difference, plainly showing,
So all, the love of Jesus, will be knowing;
That they, without excuse, receive eyes seeing
The purpose that He has for every being.

Though standing low among the throng of sinners,
Repentant hearts can turn us into winners,
Discovering our assurance in surrender,
To trust in Him, our glorious defender.

To let His Spirit fill us with such wonder,
With all our inhibitions torn asunder,
We recognise that this is now the hour
To see unleashed the fullness of His power.

His hands and feet, the time is now for walking:
The Kingdom one of power, not just talking.
Let's shine a light, and never see it faded,
The beauty of the Son no longer shaded,
His promise of new life to all revealing,
A broken land restored by Jesus' healing.

Treading Water

We're called to be a faithful son or daughter,
To give our all to God, and then some more;
Yet, far too often, we're just treading water,
When many times we should have swum to shore.

We're called to dive, with freedom unabated,
Our longing focused firmly on God's will;
Yet, somehow, when our hunger has been sated,
It is as if there's nothing left to fill.

We're called to build with more than bricks and mortar,
To rise up with the Spirit ever higher;
And yet, content to wallow, treading water,
Our hearts are dulled, instead of set on fire.

We steer away from what is really needed:
To come to a decision: sink or swim;
The hope of reaching dry land fast receded,
Resolve becomes diluted, growing dim.

Remaining undecided, muddied thinking,
For all the trees, we still can't see the wood;
While treading water, no one will be sinking,
But it's like running on the spot for good.

We're called to take no prisoners, give no quarter,
Committing all, so darkness is denied;
So, how long can we go on treading water,
Instead of swimming, surely, with the tide?

A New Friend

There are too many days I've wasted, looking far ahead,
Scared of my own shadow, fearing where things might have led,
Played it safe in mapping out the road that should be stepped,
Instead of basking in the Sun, the shadows slowly crept.
Avoiding all the challenges that I might have to face,
So fearful of the outcome of an undecided race,
Straying from the starting line, I'm watching from the stand,
Unmoved by the adventure that for me the Lord has planned,
Losing sight of what is there before my very eyes:
That every day is in itself a truly special prize.

Letting every now slip past may bring a greater cost,
For all that might be realised, the chance forever lost;
My clinging to a vision of a safely crafted morrow
Can never mitigate the risk of feeling pain and sorrow.
Unsure, still not acquiring a taste for different blends,
I hesitate to make the change, to fashion out new trends;
Hiding in the undergrowth leaves only tangled mess,
Preventing all that's still to grow, the times He longs to bless;
I need to see that here and now is where I have been planted,
That every day's a gift from God I cannot take for granted.

Yet nothing is forever, and I find I'm falling short,
The road I thought so straight may be more twisted than I thought;
It's only when I let the winds of change so freely blow
That, caution's steely rule dethroned, the days begin to flow
With all the fullness God intends that's mine to be enjoyed,
By putting all my trust in Him, my confidence is buoyed;
The obvious conclusion, that I should have known is true:
That every day is to be lived, not just for getting through.

If I instead embrace His peace and let my heart be stilled,
The things He has for me today might better be fulfilled;
Rejoicing days gone smoothly, but enduring when they're rough,
Forget tomorrow's worries, for today's will be enough;
Accept that fear for what may come will never change the end,
And contemplate the truth that every day is a new friend.

SONGS OF COMPASSION

The Lord is gracious and compassionate, slow to anger and rich in love. The Lord is good to all; he has compassion on all he has made.

Psalm 145:8-9

Reaching out

Jesus is the ultimate example of true compassion, by giving his all to free us from the slavery of our sin, choosing to die in our place.

While our own capacity for compassion may not be of the same order, we should nevertheless do the best we can, in both prayer and in action, to exercise real concern for others' troubles.

This may often call for sacrificial and selfless giving, without stopping to count how much it may cost us.

The extraordinary generosity of God's grace in all the good things that he lavishes and continues to lavish upon us, both practically and spiritually, should naturally move us to be overflowing with a desire to be as generous to others as we can possibly be.

The measure of love and mercy that we have ourselves received should spur us on to reach out to the lost and lonely, to the overlooked and marginalised, determined to draw them towards all the good things that God has to offer them.

Jesus calls us to love our neighbours; this includes not only those closest to us with whom we find it naturally easy to relate, but also to the many others beyond our immediate circle who we might otherwise simply allow to pass us by.

There is so much need in the World, and we have so many resources at our disposal that are crying out to be shared with those who are too often left wanting. A little love and compassion can go a long way.

Seen

I should have seen You on the street today,
And yet my gaze was firmly turned away;
It's always so much easier to walk by,
When I don't have to look You in the eye.

I should have marvelled at the truth You taught,
But I was too afraid of being caught,
Anticipating all that laid in store,
I'd have to share the punishment You bore.

I should have volunteered to bear your load,
Not leave You, heavy burdened, on the road
That led to your appointed dying place:
Alone, a hard and bitter end to face.

I should have stood my ground, right by your side,
Not running far away, intent to hide;
I should have been your very closest friend,
Instead of, not to know You, to pretend.

I should have been the one upon the Cross:
Instead, alone, You chose to bear my loss,
Surrendering your shattered, broken frame,
Wiped wholly clean the canvas of my shame.

So, I should see You in the poor I meet
On every corner, living on the street;
I have to grasp the need that must be fed,
So many crying out for daily bread.

And I should share the pain of the bereaved,
To walk beside the lost, so sorely grieved;
Encourage them to hear your soft voice sing,
The comfort only knowing You can bring.

I should be ready, give up pride of place,
Instead of vain ambition still to chase;
And from the treasure You bestow on me,
Share just a little, setting others free.

I need to see You: when I close my eyes,
A little more compassion in me dies;
If I could just reverse this downward trend,
Perhaps I'd take your hand, and be your friend?

Compassion

Compassion makes us open to the prompting of the Lord,
Determined that the voice of hope will never be ignored.
Compassion's more than kindness, though the two go hand in glove,
While underpinning everything should be the call of love.

Compassion leads to mercy for the lonely and the lost,
To give before receiving, without thinking of the cost.
Compassion's more than pocket change, it's giving without measure,
Content in serving those in need, surrendering our treasure.

Compassion won't be silenced, for it hangs on every word,
Ensuring that the cry for help will not be left unheard.
Compassion makes us hungry to bring others to the feast,
Without preference or favour, from the greatest to the least.

Compassion's more than generous, it brings a depth of caring,
To demonstrate the love of Christ that we are moved to sharing.
Compassion bought our freedom, when the Lord died in our place,
Our heart should be for all the World to rest within His grace.

Though undeserved, our Saviour has freed us from our mess;
As He pours out compassion, we must offer nothing less.

Unwinding

It seems like no one cares, that no one's minding
That all we once held dear is now unwinding;
We see our true perspective slowly losing,
When right and wrong are wholly of our choosing.

It's like we all have axes left for grinding;
We're searching through a maze, but never finding,
And losing all that we could once rely on:
There'll be no shoulders left for us to cry on.
When no one seems to care, when no one's minding,
It's like a book whose spine has split its binding:
The pages falling out into disorder,
No longer lining up along the border.

When no one's taking care in what they're doing,
Our focus wholly on our dreams pursuing;
Though driving on, without a thought of pausing,
We can't ignore the wreckage that we're causing.
Though deafened by a plethora of voices,
Convincing us we have so many choices,
With all too many boundaries eroding,
Our souls too soon are captured by foreboding.

We have to show we care, that we are minding,
And not allow the darkness to be blinding
So many from a truth that's worth the knowing:
That there remains a different light that's glowing,
To point them back towards the path they're made for,
The toll already satisfied, and paid for.
When we speak out, God's love and grace for sharing,
Perhaps some may decide it is worth caring:
And if, with His, their hearts are moved to binding,
We might see just a little less unwinding.

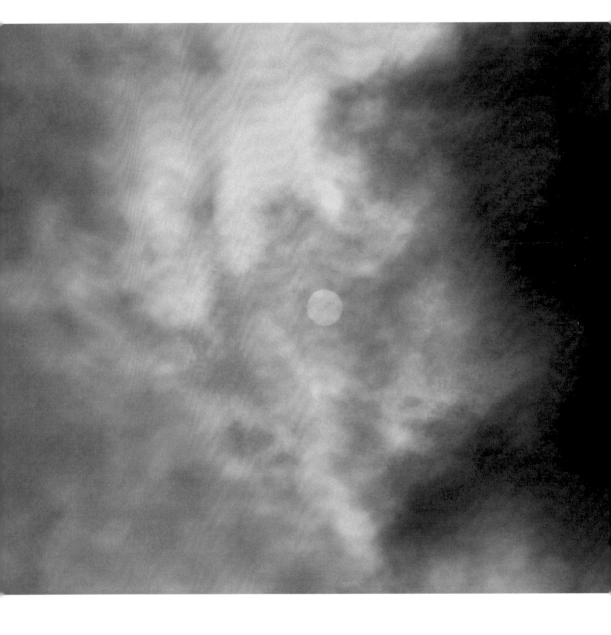

SONGS OF DOUBT

Then Jesus told [Thomas], "Because you have seen me, you have believed; blessed are those who have not seen and yet have believed."

John 20:29

Overcoming doubt

The Bible urges us to put aside our uncertainties and to trust in the promises of God, but it also encourages us to be merciful to those who experience doubt.

In times of trouble and adversity, it is only natural to have doubts; doubts before coming to faith and doubts even after coming to know God in a way that is only possible by accepting and trusting in Jesus as our personal Saviour.

The key is not to let doubts overwhelm us, but to bring them, honestly, and openly, to God and to ask him to deal with them – and he will.

The more we come to develop a closer and more trusting personal relationship with Jesus, the less power doubt will hold over us.

But it does not mean that we will never find ourselves without questions or uncertainties. When we do, we should hold fast to the fact that God understands our weaknesses and is always there to reassure us, ready to journey with us and to help us overcome the challenges that we face.

Some may say that it is wrong for people of faith to doubt. On the contrary, surely it is only human…?

Still Thomas, I

I see your hand in everything you do,
For so much good can only come from You –
A testimony that your love is true:
And yet – despite this – still I question why.
You shower me in blessings without count,
Provide for me in more than full amount,
Your love for me an ever-flowing fount;
And yet – despite it all – still Thomas, I.

I sense your presence in the calm and still
Of prayer, and that You answer as You will,
And graciously supply me with my fill;
And yet – the call for proof remains my cry.
My life transformed in ways I couldn't see,
Your awesome sacrifice to set me free,
You gave your all because You first loved me;
And yet – despite it all – still Thomas, I.

Your Spirit, through your grace, for me You leave,
How happy I should be when I receive,
Although I have not seen, I yet believe;
Yet, sometimes, still my human doubts defy.
Though in my heart I've touched your wounds that bleed,
And know by this from death's dark power I'm freed,
That proof beyond this faith I should not need:
Sometimes, despite it all, still Thomas, I.

Doubting

Doubt is a natural process;
Hope reduced by fears
Is not a cause to be ashamed;
Our faith allows for tears.

Doubting isn't disbelieving,
It's just believing less;
For a moment, wavering,
And moved to second guess.

Doubting may lead to contention,
But still, God hears us speak,
Responds to our every question,
Accepting we are weak.

Doubting shows our limitations:
But, in our hearts, we know
Seeking Him for resolution
Will help our faith to grow.

Doubting points us to a tide
Against which we can't swim;
All our trust and certainty
Are only found in Him.

Doubting we can't fix ourselves,
Leaves nothing left to prove;
Putting our lives in Jesus' hands
Will let the Spirit move.

God wants us to be real with Him:
There is no guilt in doubt;
For when we seek Him truthfully
His love will work it out.

Remember

When doubters said: 'it can't be done',
God proved them wrong, He sent His Son;
When only total love would do,
He paid the price and saw it through.

When doubters said: 'he's nothing more
Than prophets we have heard before',
His words cried out as God's alone,
Through acts of love and power shown.
The lame to walk, the blind to see,
A pointer to eternity;
The dead revived, to breathe once more,
A foretaste of what lay in store.

When doubters said 'there's no way back',
He took, instead, a different track;
'Yet not my will, but yours' he said,
Prepared to number with the dead.
Too easy to just walk away,
He chose, instead, to seize the day;
Like falling drops of blood, the sweat
And tears, to meet our greatest debt.

When doubters said 'it's all too much,
Where now the healer's saving touch?'
He chose to set aside His gain,
'Mine not to test', His sure refrain.

When doubters said 'the cost's too high'
He paid the price, prepared to die,
He knew it was the only way
To bring us our salvation day.

When doubters said 'his time is done',
He knew that it had just begun;
The grave could not contain Him long:
His resurrection proved them wrong.

When doubters tell you nothing's there,
That prayers 'just fade into thin air',
Remember that He too was mocked,
So many times His message blocked.
Remember that His promise stands,
When we hold fast to His commands;
Through faith and trust, He saw it through,
Completing all God called Him to.

So, put aside all lingering doubt,
Proclaim the Lord with joyful shout:
Through Him all things are truly done,
In Him, eternal life is won!

Songs of Freedom

Jesus said, "If you hold to my teaching, you are really my disciples. Then you will know the truth, and the truth will set you free… if the Son sets you free, you will be free indeed."

John 8:31-32, 36

Jesus answered, "I am the way and the truth and the life. No-one comes to the Father except through me. If you really knew me, you would know my Father as well."

John 14:6-7

Loosing the chains

There are so many things that can limit and restrict our ability to enjoy life to the full. We may be held captive by the impact of past experiences, hurts and regrets; by difficult situations and relationships that we currently find ourselves in; or by concerns and fears for what the future may bring.

Brokenness in our own lives and fractured relationships with others may weigh heavily and painfully upon us and can be difficult to cast off.

Jesus is the answer to our longing for freedom from all that troubles us and holds us down, if we are ready to seek his help. He promises that he is the truth that has come to set us free and to restore our relationship with God and, through that, with those around us.

With what freedoms are followers of Jesus blessed?

Accepting Jesus as our Saviour and as Lord of our lives frees us from the pressures of the World around us. We are made free to have a personal relationship with God, with direct access to his Holy Spirit; free from the slavery of sin and death; free to love others as Jesus loves us; and free to be the people that God has made us to be.

Liberty or captivity? The choice is ours to make.

Coming Clean

The time has come for waking from this never-ending dream,
Despite my every effort, I am running out of steam;
I need to lose the notion that I'm somehow in control,
That it is wholly in my strength that I can make me whole;
The battery is fading, as my light is growing dim:
I have to put myself aside, and find my way to Him.

I know where He can take me, but remembering where I've been,
I need to face up to the truth, it's time for coming clean:
Too often I have walked a path made not by Him, but me,
By vainly thinking this the only way to set me free;
But every blind alley leads to just the next brick wall,
Too high for me to ever scale, still set to take the fall.

I want to seize the future now, not living in the past,
To cling to something hopeful, that is really made to last;
To walk the way that He directs, delivering the plan
That He had put in place for me before the World began.

I want to spend forever in the presence of the Lord,
Walking in the cool of day, with every good thing stored;
Returning to that perfect place, where I was made to be,
Knowing deep within my soul He's always there for me.

I want to be a follower and, letting Jesus lead,
Have confidence that He alone can give me all I need;
Forgetting my agenda, I just want to hear His voice,
That points me to a better way, that guards my every choice.

I want to find humility, instead of standing proud,
To recognise it's Jesus who should stand out from the crowd;
To always put His glory first, discarding all of mine,
Contented with the place I have, the last one in the line.

I want to let Him take my dark, and turn it into light,
To set aside my every wrong, to make my living right;
The stage is set and ready for delivering the scene,
Where, by the grace of God, I may at last be coming clean.

Unchained

When it feels like a prison cell is what our life's become,
When chasing things that have no worth has only left us numb,
The bondage of the World may seem too often unrestrained:
But, breaking through the barriers, God's Word is never chained.

When we are sold the story that it's this life, and no more,
By those whose hearts are blinded to what really lies in store,
The powers of the World may try to spin contrary tales:
But, breaking through the lines, the truth of Jesus Christ prevails.

When plants put into shallow ground too soon begin to flake,
And thorns contrive to choke the growth that we had hoped to make;
The lure of worldly promises may weave a tangled mess:
But, breaking through the briars, God's seed can flourish nonetheless.

When we resolve to put God first, our lives to His subsume,
If we let Jesus have His way, His promise in full bloom,
He will return us home, though we were lost and gone astray:
The unchained glory of the Lord will have the final say.

Idols

When I look to the World for my needing,
With my focus on Heaven receding,
When prosperity's comfort enfolds me,
I lose sight of the Saviour who holds me.

My faithfulness measured in fractions,
When I'm sidetracked by worthless distractions,
When I seek nothing more than my pleasure,
Empty nothings unworthy to treasure.

With my thinking again turned to leading
That my own strength is all that I'm needing,
It's small wonder, and not unexpected,
That the Spirit of Truth is neglected.

In trying to write my own story,
Instead of exalting His glory,
My finely clothed prayers left in tatters,
When I lose sight of what really matters.

Yet, it's just when my longing is ceasing,
That my praise should be ever increasing,
By humbly recalling, confessing
The wonders of every past blessing.

It must never be taken for granted,
The incredible seed that is planted;
Every day I should let it astound me
That the Maker of all sought and found me.
For without His great love and forgiving,
Life is not worth a moment of living.

The Captive Past

Yesterday, seen through our rose-tinted glasses,
Can look so much better, the more time that passes;
We walked on the water, our feet barely wet,
Convinced all our longings were perfectly met.

But being beholden to things of the past,
May see the ship sink while we cling to the mast;
An uncharted course will not keep us afloat,
When we're lacking the will to step out of the boat.

If we stand in its wake, if the waves rise unchecked,
It may blow us off course, on the rocks to be wrecked;
But when we're assured that the Lord leads us through
We can sail with assurance a course that is new.

Though nostalgia, as sharp as a true two-edged sword,
Can at once seem secure, yet cut clean through the cord,
Still, the things from before can be used to inspire,
To recall where we've come from, but aim even higher.

We may draw on the past, but the future is now,
We can walk with the Lord if we let Him show how;
This, the insight we need, yet so easily lack;
The clock only runs forward, it never goes back.

Believe

It really could have saved us so much grief,
To recognise that worry is a thief;
Accepting that our days won't look so grim,
When we decide to cast our cares on Him.

The World may try to hold us in its thrall,
Suggesting that we're not so good at all,
The course so surely charted, hard to swerve;
Convicted it's no more than we deserve,
That there is no one else to take the blame:
Too quick to simply wallow in our shame.

Though life may sometimes seem a losing fight,
That all our troubles have the sharpest bite,
With God on board, the dragon has no teeth,
We need not fear what seems to lie beneath;
Instead, to rest in Him should be our all:
He holds us up, and will not let us fall.

It's something all along we should have known,
  That we don't have to face our trials alone;
  We're not a people made to bear such pain,
  Without someone to help us take the strain.

Each day may have its own sufficient woe,
  And yet His care is all we need to know;
  We're out of stock, with only empty shelves,
  We're called to look so far beyond our selves:
    His precious gift, be ready to receive,
    It's all He asks: to trust and to believe.

SONGS OF INTEGRITY

[Jesus said] "Do not judge, or you too will be judged. For in the same way as you judge others, you will be judged, and with the measure you use, it will be measured to you."

Matthew 7:1-2

Living out faith

As flawed and weak human beings, our failure fully to live out and model a Christian life may understandably lead to charges of hypocrisy.

For sure, faith in Jesus does not make us impervious to the temptations of the World. But it should make us more aware of the ease with which we can succumb to thoughts, attitudes and behaviours that will lead us away from God.

We should be slow to criticise what we perceive to be the shortcomings of others, as we come to realise the extent of our own failings. An honest assessment of ourselves will only too soon show just how unqualified we are to stand in judgment on anyone. Only God is righteous; justice belongs to him.

We can, of course, only give the best we have, and day to day, with God's help, aspire to be better than before, as we journey with him towards our ultimate destination, when we will be fully restored in the new Heaven and the new Earth.

We must be praying at all times for God's strength to rise to the challenge, so that with his help we might take a different course.

Judged

Too quick to see the fault outside,
With my own failings left denied,
Self-satisfied, I call the tune,
Condemning others' wrongs too soon.

Yet this is but a facile screen,
To keep my sin from being seen;
My heart should be to set things right,
Before I look to take the fight
To others, coming clean with God,
Confessing every path untrod,
Where I have fallen so far short,
In traps of my own making caught.

It's only Jesus' grace that frees:
I should be daily on my knees,
Acknowledging the much I lack,
To let my Saviour lead me back
To where He calls me to be found:
Feet firmly set on solid ground.

Mine not to judge, but simply serve,
And from His ways to never swerve;
Equipped to follow where He leads,
To minister to others' needs,
Reliant not on what I've done,
But wholly on the Father's Son;
It's then the lost I'll see Him bring,
To bow before Him as their King.

Alone, all I might do or say
Will of itself not win the day;
I need His hand to wipe the stain,
To see God's love and mercy reign,
To let my sense of judgment dim:
Accepting justice rests with Him.

Who am I to stand as judge,
When my own fault I try to fudge?
A full confession I must own,
That I might sound a different tone,
So those outside may make the choice,
Not hearing mine, but His sweet voice,
That calls for lives to rearrange:
It's then I'll see a real change.

Glass Houses

It's easy, in self-righteousness, to sit upon our throne;
Our hand is far too ready to be casting the first stone.
To hold ourselves examples of the way that all should live,
Ignores our own shortcomings that we need God to forgive.

We set a higher standard than we'd ever hope to reach;
Our words expose the truth that we don't practise what we preach.
We cannot take the higher ground, our starting point so low:
For we have fallen so far short and let the distance grow.

The speck within another's eye, too quickly we reprove,
While there's a plank within our own that we have still to move.
Though hard to find such wisdom, to admit where we've gone wrong,
Resistance to repentance finds us out before too long.

As we'd have others do for us, we're called to do the same;
For we are just as broken, with an equal share of blame.
Though feeling wholly slighted, still, we have to let it pass;
For stones should not be thrown by those with houses made of glass.

Bread

Unmoved, and yet it should have made me cry,
When I saw Jesus begging in the street, but passed Him by;
When Jesus asked for just one piece of bread,
I held it back for me alone, consumed it all instead.

When Jesus lay in chains by prison wall,
I threw away the key and blocked my ears to every call;
Though I saw Jesus battered, torn and bruised,
I turned my gaze aside, to go the extra mile refused,
To help Him in His greatest hour of need
Completely failed; on that cruel Cross I left Him there to bleed.

Unmoved, as if I didn't care at all
When I saw Jesus all alone, I didn't make the call
That might have brought at least some small relief,
Untended, unresponsive to His loneliness and grief.

Yet though I leave Him, hanging on the tree,
Each time ignoring others' needs, I think of only me,
In mercy He forgives my everything,
He suffers in my place, removes the power of death's dark sting.

So, when I see the hurting and the lost,
He calls me to remember I was bought at such a cost,
That if in Him I truly want to live,
There's so much more that I've received that I must choose to give.

Too long has my indifference increased;
If I could learn to see Him in the weakest and the least,
Perhaps then I might really make a start,
To open wide my arms, submit, and crucify my heart.

Practice

I wondered:
What heights I might have reached,
If I'd practised what I preached;
If I'd let my heart be stirred
With the depth of God's true Word,
If the promises I'd spoken
Were fulfilled, and not just token.

I considered:
What more I might have made
If upon His path I'd stayed;
Just how much could have been changed
If my heart was rearranged
In the face of Heaven's love
With perspective from above;
What a wondrous sight to see,
How He gave His all for me.

I questioned:
If it's possible to become
Parts that make a greater sum,
Letting Him pull me together,
To push on through stormy weather;
If I gave Him all my trust,
As I surely know I must,
How much more might then be seen
Of the man I should have been?

Still, I wondered:
What change I might have made
If more fervently I prayed;
Transformation undelivered
When I let my heart be quivered,
When I let fear have its day,
Get too often in the way
Of the road that's mine for walking,
When my feet should do the talking.

I reflected:
While I live, it's not too late
To pursue a better state
That He longs to build in me;
To become His hands and feet,
In a World that owns retreat;
If I let myself be brave,
Just how many could He save
Who would otherwise be lost;
I must look to pay the cost,
When I'm swallowing my pride,
Setting selfish ways aside;
If to be last in the queue
Is the first I seek to do,
Putting others' needs ahead,
Doing what I once just said,
All the walls that would be breached:
If I'd practised what I preached.

Then I pondered:
There's no longer time to wait,
To go through that narrow gate;
If I let Him hold the door,
There's an invitation sure
That He's making ever known;
If I let His truth be shown
In my actions, not just voice,
Helping others make their choice,
The reality of living
In the fullness God is giving,
Then, at last, instead of falling,
I might hear Him clearly calling
And His true desire reach,
When I practise what I preach.

SONGS OF PERSEVERANCE

[Jesus said] "…All men will hate you because of me, but he who stands firm to the end will be saved…"

Mark 13:13

…we also rejoice in our sufferings, because we know that suffering produces perseverance; perseverance, character; and character, hope. And hope does not disappoint us, because God has poured out his love into our hearts by the Holy Spirit, whom he has given us.

Romans 5:3-5

Keep on keeping on

In the Christian life, we are called to 'run with perseverance the race marked out for us' (Hebrews 12:1).

The way of living that God calls us to embrace requires endurance, determination, and persistence on our part; we must be prepared to be in it for the long haul.

This will not be without its challenges and we must expect to face sometimes fierce resistance, scorn, insult, and even outright rejection, by a World determined to run an entirely different sort of race to our own.

The temptation for us is to follow the path of least resistance, putting challenges aside, giving in too readily when things get tough, content to settle for so much less than God intends for us.

Anything of lasting value and true satisfaction requires real effort. But we are not alone; we can stand up and be counted, confident that Jesus stands with us, walks beside us and equips us with all we need for the journey. When we learn to trust in his amazing provision, we can overcome many of the hurdles that we will inevitably encounter along the way.

We can take great comfort in being assured that we are held by a love that forever perseveres: the depth of God's love for us helps us to keep going, no matter what life may bring.

Jesus is so much greater than we are; he will uphold us through our trials and reward our perseverance. With him by our side, everything changes. We view the challenges that we face from an entirely new perspective; and we find ourselves being changed, as he uses those trials to build up our character and our hope.

We may be fickle and inconstant, but Jesus is faithful. He guarantees to deliver of his best to those who persevere, who hold fast and trust in his plans, waiting in patient expectation for better things to come.

Mess

It's not a bed of roses, life's not always what we hope:
When things get hard and weigh us down, when it's so hard to cope;
It feels like all we have is just a daily S.O.S.,
When nothing's ever simple, in the muddle and the mess.

Though briars and thorns entangle us and all too sharply tear,
Still, we can rest assured it won't be more than we can bear;
And though on rocky paths our seed may often seem to fall,
Blown by the winds assailing us, and not take root at all,
By trusting God's provision, we discover new ways found
For nurturing our love and faith, alive in fertile ground.

Though it may seem we're caught up in a web of our own making,
With indecision taking hold, resolve so close to breaking,
The Lord is there to rescue us, He always hears our cry,
And He will surely free us, set us loose again to fly.

While still this side of Heaven, we may fear there is so much
Left in a state of turmoil, damaged by the human touch;
Where trouble lies before us, everything seems out of place:
Still, all will be restored when we meet Jesus face to face.

But, until then, we can be sure there's One who understands
Our doubts and our uncertainties throughout life's shifting sands;
He knows so well our every pain, our longing and distress:
Our God is always with us, in the muddle and the mess.

Heartbeat

When I'm standing too still, when my breathing is shallow,
There'll be little produced and the field remains fallow;
When I'm still hesitating, He calls me to action,
That I might push on and at last gain some traction.

With my heart beating louder, I pick up the pace,
And my pulse rate is rising, beginning to race;
When it seems any moment control could be lost,
I am tempted to wonder: 'is this worth the cost?'

But then He reassures me that all will come good
If I follow His lead, as I know that I should;
That whatever I face, every bump in the road,
He'll be right there beside me, supporting the load.

When He is returning me back to the start,
His finger once more on the pulse of my heart,
Recalling my first love when faith came alive,
Then my passion to serve can do more than survive.

What a wonder to know that the Lord of Creation
Who exchanged Heaven's heights for the lowliest station,
Who by sacrifice no greater love could have shown,
Bids me walk in His footsteps as one of His own.

So, I step out in faith, as I trust Him to lead,
Letting Jesus equip me with all that I need;
For He's known me and knows me more than I can say,
And His heart beats for mine, as He shows me the way.

With God at Our Side

When out of our comfort we find ourselves shaken,
And from our soul's slumber we finally awaken,
To walk the new road that God asks to be taken:
We will find that we forfeit the World's lasting favour.
Becoming, like Him, a rejected pariah,
For the price that He paid could not be any higher,
And we too may be led to endure through the fire;
Still, His Spirit ensures we'll not falter or waver.

When we are insulted without justification,
When the lies that are spoken see only inflation,
When we find ourselves strangers within our own nation:
We take comfort that Jesus endured this the same.
Although battered and bruised, He chose not to surrender
To hatred, instead reaching out with love, tender,
Unhesitating, His own life to render,
That all might be saved by the power of His name.

When we stand on His Word, with our faith ever growing,
We have such a great hope, and a certainty, knowing
The assurance of where He has promised we're going:
While we're holding on fast, we cannot be denied.
Despite so many barbs that are seeking to tear us,
The shouts of the World, pressing in, cannot scare us,
For His love and His mercy will ever prepare us:
We can scale any mountain with God at our side!

Jericho

When we're facing our own Jericho,
Will we hold back, or go with the flow?
Will we blow on our trumpets, so loud,
Or fade, silently, into the crowd?

Will our banners be waving so high,
Led by Him, so our feet remain dry,
Cross the waters, by letting Him lead?
Faith in Jesus is all that we need.

Though the challenges faced seem so great,
He assures us it's not time to wait,
If we hold to the promise He's made,
There's no raining upon our parade.

If we take Him in trust at His word,
By the call of the Lord deeply stirred,
Knowing He has left nothing to chance,
In true faith we can lead the advance.

Though the outcome we cannot see yet,
All the plans of the Lord will be met,
To rely on the move of His power,
We will see greater confidence flower.

God's strong hand hems the enemy in,
To resist Him they cannot begin;
For the seeds of His triumph are sown
As the trumpets are faithfully blown.

So, let's press on and break down the walls,
Storming through as the citadel falls,
As the Lord gives us victory won,
For the glory of God's only Son!

Storm Clouds

The Sun doesn't shine quite as much as it used to,
The storm clouds are gathering every day;
The crosswinds grow stronger and threaten to break us,
The direction of travel increasingly grey.

The light and the darkness no longer seem equals,
We seem to be stuck on a long losing streak;
The descent ever steeper, where once there was turning,
The prospects for change look increasingly bleak.

The news that assails us from every quarter
Is pressing us down and unfailingly grim;
With even a glimmer of light hard to fashion,
Recovery's hope seems increasingly slim.

Relying upon what the World has to offer:
Plants in soil that is arid, with withering shoots,
Standing our ground, with no prospect of growing,
Will not help us rise, but torn up at the roots.

It is only by seeing the past as our future,
Recognising our need to return to the start,
That there's only one garden for us to return to,
Our true balance restored, with the Lord at its heart.

For the light that He offers dispels every darkness,
With heaviness lifted, the skies become clear;
If we look to the heavens and follow His leading,
Then the end of our turmoil will grow ever near.

When we're walking with God, there's a peace that will settle,
Once again, in the cool of the day, by our side,
And the light that He shines that illumes us forever,
Not a cloud in the sky will be able to hide.

Though there may be such weight that the days pile upon us,
When we hold to the victory that Jesus has won,
The storm clouds replaced by a day ever lighter:
Our future shines bright in the face of the Son.

Songs of the Lost

[Jesus said], "Then the righteous will answer him, 'Lord, when did we see you hungry and feed you, or thirsty and give you something to drink?'... The King will reply, 'I tell you the truth, whatever you did for one of the least of these brothers of mine, you did for me.'..."

Matthew 25:37, 40

Suppose a brother or sister is without clothes and daily food. If one of you says to him, "Go, I wish you well; keep warm and well fed," but does nothing about his physical needs, what good is it? In the same way, faith by itself, if it is not accompanied by action, is dead.

James 2:15-17

Lost and found

We live in a world of plenty, but a world that is increasingly wasteful.

We have at our disposal an abundance of natural resources, such that no one should go hungry and none should be in want of the basic essentials of life: food, clothing and shelter.

Yet, even in our extraordinarily prosperous Western world, there are countless numbers of our fellow human beings whom we have simply allowed to fall off the edge of the regular, organised, society that we so cherish and in which we take such pride.

These lost souls do little more than exist on the streets of our towns and cities, in a fragile and perilous state, under our very noses. They are clearly visible, yet for all practical purposes unseen, as we go about our daily business, ignoring a need that could so easily be met.

In a supreme irony, the discarded packaging, from which we greedily pull the meaningless artifacts with which we fill our empty lives, often become the very homes of those whom we pass by.

Throughout his ministry, time and again Jesus modelled compassion for the poor, the dispossessed and the hungry. If we are to follow his example, our profession of faith must be matched by positive action, with a readiness to help those least able to help themselves. As Christians, it should be our natural inclination to make a real difference to the communities in which we live, and in particular to reach out to those who are poorest and most disadvantaged.

It is sometimes overlooked that the Christian Church does already make an enormous contribution to the social and economic wellbeing of the Nation, through the vast array of charitable services provided by an army of dedicated volunteers. Christian charities often 'fill the gaps' when the social welfare system has been unable to do so.

But there will always be so much more to do. How easily do we close our eyes (and our hearts) to the need that is all around us…?

The Cardboard Box Brigade

The night springs swiftly from its lair,
The wind flings shards of icy air;
As darkness comes, the cold night hardens,
Moonlight gleams on ice in gardens.
But in the fields, below the trees,
The sleepers face another freeze –
With wooden pillows for their heads,
Discarded packaging their beds,
Their hope is not for sleep arrive,
But just another night survive:
The sadness of the World displayed
In the cardboard box brigade.

And while they sleep in fitful mood,
Deprived of shelter, warmth and food,
Like driftwood nudging at the shore,
The debris of what was before,
We look, and yet we do not see
The blot upon the scenery;
Our hearts reject the silent cry,
No Good Samaritan passes by.
We take it not as our concern,
And simply never choose to learn
The kind of future we have made
For the cardboard box brigade.

The cold of night grows ever deep,
Dispensing more than merely sleep,
And somewhere in that lost brigade
A withered spark begins to fade.
The cold wind blows, with final shout,
The vestiges of living out,
As time has run the course allowed,
His paper home becomes a shroud.
His parting passes us, unseen,
It is as if he'd never been:
Just one less Private on parade
In the cardboard box brigade.

Front Line

His home is a blanket that's tattered and torn,
So old it was made long before he was born.
A hard concrete slab on a non-descript street,
No comfort, no shelter, no place to retreat.

Though thousands pass by, he's completely unknown;
A line has been drawn, he must hold it alone.
Ignored, and unseen by unpitying eyes
Whose focus is on such a different prize.
Alone, on an island that nobody knows,
Around which the throng of humanity flows,
A place so remote, it is lost without trace
From our blinkered view; only he knows his place.

His home is a darkness returning too soon,
As the sunlight surrenders the sky to the Moon.
There is no reprieve as the night time descends
And sleep – if it comes – is the greatest of friends.
Yet he lives with a sadness entrenched and so deep,
It continues to haunt, even when he's asleep;
His awakening offers an unwelcome dawn
Of a future whose prospects are ever forlorn.

He's fighting a battle that cannot be won,
Defeat is assured long before it's begun;
Unthinking dullness his only retreat
From the depths of despair in this life on the street.

He inhabits a world we exclude from our sight,
Denying we have any part in his plight.
Too close for our comfort, we simply deny,
But each step that we take lends more truth to the lie.

All that he is, on the brink of collapse
That is only held off by his begging for scraps,
To stave off an ending that none could have planned,
In hopelessness, making this one, final stand.

His home has a name that's a desperate plea,
That most, passing by, would prefer not to see.
His humble request just to 'give what you can';
Without it, he's lost: he has no other plan.

Desire Unbroken

Can your will be done, with my willingness jaded,
My ardour initial, yet easily faded?
Faith without action, in practice a token,
My failure to share leaves the truth still unspoken.

A spark to a flame could be burning so brightly,
The glow is suppressed by my holding too tightly;
My passion snuffed out before even starting,
Intent and delivery easily parting.

So, passing on by, opportunities flowing
Remain unfulfilled, my desire unshowing.
I hide in my shell, hesitation not cracking,
Accepting as normal, a boldness that's lacking.

You're there to be seen, but it's me that won't let it,
My comfort, too great, for the risk, to upset it;
Hands deep in my pockets, determined, unmoving,
Inertia a state all too readily proving.
Collar up, eyes turned down, I pass by without seeing
The chains I could break, of the ones I'd be freeing;
I go on my way, in the other direction,
Denying the truth, in my selfish rejection.

If I just let His promptings assure me of knowing
There's a new destination where I should be going;
If, instead, I looked up, hands held wide for His gifting,
To rescue the lost, all who see Him, uplifting,
I'd walk in His footsteps, the path mine to follow,
Then all I profess wouldn't seem quite so hollow;
For it's only in doing, the truth will be heard,
My actions speak louder than every word.

So where is the courage that should have been mine
From the moment I saw water turned into wine;
From the time I first heard that sweet voice in my soul,
That offered the promise of making me whole;
From the flowing of tongues from my lips, yet unknown,
For the years He's been faithful, the love that He's shown?

Can I go on, half-hearted, with lukewarm desire,
Stepping out just so far, before dowsing the fire?
If I truly am His, both His hands and His feet,
Let me walk in His way, 'till we finally meet!

SONGS FOR A TIME YET TO COME
PART 4: THE MERCIFUL GOD

Songs of Contrition

The sacrifices of God are a broken spirit; a broken and contrite heart, O God, you will not despise.

Psalm 51:17

Godly sorrow brings repentance that leads to salvation and leaves no regret, but worldly sorrow brings death.

2 Corinthians 7:10

Job done?

For a Christian, that the power of death has been forever conquered by Christ's sacrifice on the Cross is not at issue: as Scripture says, he 'died to sin once for all' (Romans 6:10).

But that does not mean that we can just sit back and revel in the extraordinary gift of grace freely given to us, in spite of our otherwise perilous state.

On the contrary, if we are to respond appropriately to such a gift, we should constantly be aiming to move away from those patterns of behaviour, thoughts, attitudes and actions that offend God's plan for our lives.

Repentance is not simply about saying sorry. It is far more than that: true repentance calls for complete rejection of the sins that can so easily infect our lives. It requires us to make a 180-degree turn; and to have a determined resolution to head in the opposite direction.

This requires perseverance on our part; and an understanding that it is, and will remain, an ongoing process for the rest of our time on Earth. But with God's help, we can do it.

Jesus feels the pain we cause when we fail to treat others with love and respect; when we ride roughshod over their feelings, hopes and aspirations; when we selfishly guard our possessions to ourselves; when we allow avarice, greed and jealousy to overcome our better nature.

In this sense at least, every time that we fail him, it is as if we put him back on the Cross and drive the nails in once more. We should never lose sight of the fact that it is to atone for all of our sins, past, present and future, that he endured the ultimate sacrifice for us; and that the salvation that his sacrifice offers is available to all who choose to believe and trust in him.

The good news is that even when we do recognise our true state, we are not condemned to wallow in the depths of shame or regret. Because of Jesus' sacrifice, we can rejoice that we are forgiven and accepted unconditionally by our loving Creator.

Job done? By God, yes; by us, not by a long way…

Contrition

True faith offers trust without seeing it all,
Taking God at His word, He will not let us fall.
But to rise from the darkness to glorious light
We have to be humble, and broken, contrite.

We can't make it alone, all our efforts are naught,
Elusive, the freedom so long we have sought;
Yet the burdens we carry have soon taken flight
When we come in humility, broken, contrite.

The blessings abound that He wants us to hear,
When we follow His will, then He truly draws near.
But He doesn't want prayers that are too lightly spoken,
He is seeking a heart that is contrite and broken.

From the weight of our sin we are lifted and freed
When we fall to our knees and confess every need.
But He wants true repentance and not a mere token,
A soul in humility, contrite and broken.

He seeks transformation in every part,
If we just let Him in to the depths of our heart.
He is longing to see that real change has awoken
In a spirit that's humble, and contrite and broken.

Surrendered completely, in deepest contrition,
To offer our all, this should be our ambition.
Open to Him, as our spirit is stirred,
To seek out our calling and follow His Word.
To embrace what was won when our Saviour died,
And into His keep let our whole selves confide;
To receive all the blessings that Jesus has spoken,
For hearts that are humbled, and contrite and broken.

Repentance

If we let the past rule us, still held in its thrall,
We will not find redemption, we're certain to fall;
Holding onto resentment brings nothing but loss,
Denying the price paid so dear at the Cross.

Remembering God's mercy should stir us to love,
As the Spirit of Jesus descends like a dove;
When our own self-importance we learn to disown,
Real desire for forgiveness begins to be grown.

Like starting to speak, but not ending the sentence
Is regret that is shallow, that lacks true repentance;
Words alone bring no closure, without giving more,
Old wounds are left festering, open and sore.

It's more than about just admitting our wrong,
We have to rewrite every line of the song,
Striking a chord with a different inflection,
The melody taking a whole new direction.

We have to move on to arrive somewhere new,
To let go of past hurts, reconstruction pursue;
With the Lord as our driver, our pilot, our guide,
We discover real turning, deep rooted inside.

Words aren't enough, they must be matched by action
If a change in our heart is to really gain traction,
Confess like we mean it and do as we pray,
Take a truly new path, made anew every day!

Regret

Regret will never give you what you lack,
Regret won't take you forward, only back;
Regretting just weighs heavy, like a stone
And can't relieve the pain that you have known.

Regret will keep you prisoner to the last,
And it can never mend a broken past;
It won't put fallen fruit back on the tree,
Regret will hold you back from being free.

Regret will fester, like an open wound,
And, like the shipwrecked, you will feel marooned,
Left on a desert island without friends,
A message in a bottle no one sends.

Regret knows how to capture you too well,
Of your own making, locks you in a cell;
Regret will tie your hands, and bind your heart;
While it persists, there can be no new start.

Regret must be resisted at each turn,
Its naked flame must not be left to burn;
What's passed left in the past, not kept alive,
With not a single vestige to survive.

What might have been is never ours to know,
What was can't be undone, just let it go,
Resolved that out of sight is out of mind,
To draw a line across what's left behind,
Will let you pass on fruitfully instead,
And look towards a brighter day ahead;
So, give it back to God, who knows you best:
Put trust in Him, and He will give you rest.

Dwell

Hindsight, it's said, is a wonderful thing,
We can look back on years with a different eye;
Yet, despite all the clarity ageing might bring,
We can't change the past, even though we may try.

Were we on the right track for all of those years,
Or was it just a treadmill we stumbled upon,
As we worked the machine, going up through the gears,
Any thought of reverse very soon would be gone?

We pressed on, unthinkingly, mile followed mile,
The chances to step off were few and between;
And the times we might stop lasted only a while,
As our eyes remained closed, letting them pass, unseen.

We wonder what might have been, if we'd been bolder,
If we'd been brave and stepped out of the boat;
If we'd not given every new thing the cold shoulder,
Neither sinking nor swimming, but fudging the vote.

If we'd seen all we knew as a fair-weather friend,
If we'd ridden the waves and sailed through deeper waters,
Would we have discovered a different end,
Like some new arrival, to take up new quarters?

It just serves us ill, all this empty reflection;
Though we are where we are, moving forward brings chances
To shake off the weight of this dull introspection,
Instead, learning steps for more challenging dances.

No longer contained, there's a skin for the shedding,
Escaping the loop of a constant repeat;
It's never too late for new paths to be treading,
To march to the sound of a different beat.

When lost on the margins, He will realign us,
While marking what's done, setting out for the new;
The past gives perspective, but shouldn't define us,
The future's unwritten, so much left to do.

The past is a place not for dwelling too long,
Close the door on regret and accept God's forgiving;
We should seek out new rhythms, a different song,
Stepping out, without fear, to a new way of living.

With an ear to the ground and a heart that is willing,
We can dust ourselves off and get ready to fly,
Taking hold of a hope that is truly fulfilling:
The only way up, when on God we rely.

Beside the Door

'I stood beside the door, to let you in;
You gave no thanks, I took it on the chin,
Attended to your coming and your going,
Like one unseen, who wasn't worth the knowing.'

'I took your coat, I wiped your muddy boots,
But it was plain you didn't give two hoots
For all my efforts, still, taken for granted:
A nobody, so easily supplanted.'

'I watched your things, while you were busy eating,
Ensured your every need, so surely meeting;
Gave all I had, yet showed no indignation
That you would leave me in the lowest station.'

'You took your hat from me as you were leaving,
I stood, without a word of thanks receiving;
I wondered if you really hadn't seen me,
And how you might have felt if you had been me.'

'No matter all the times that you ignore me,
And though it seems you're doing nothing for me,
Just like the very first time that I saw you,
My call remains to keep on rooting for you.'

'For just a while you thought me some messiah,
But just as soon portrayed me as a liar:
"We don't believe that he's the one who frees us:
Who does he think he is, this man called Jesus?"'

'So, as the door is closed, once more, behind you,
I wonder what I have to do to find you;
But I will stand my ground, not hesitating:
For every soul that's saved is worth the waiting.'

SONGS OF FAITH

Now faith is being sure of what we hope for and certain of what we do not see.

Hebrews 11:1

Deciding to believe

Faith is a decision.

Christian faith requires that we decide to believe in the truth, as revealed in the Bible, about who Jesus Christ is and to believe in his power to redeem and to restore us to be the people that God made us to be.

There are challenges in making that decision: not least, accepting the changes that will inevitably have to be made to our attitudes and patterns of living. In a World where we are encouraged from the earliest years to be self-sufficient and to believe that if we do not look after number one, no one else will, this means being willing to give up control and put our fate wholly into the hands of someone else.

It is perhaps only when we come to understand that the someone else is the Creator of everything and, moreover, someone who has demonstrated in the clearest and most dramatic way that he loves and cares for each one of us far beyond all human measure, that we can start to '...trust in the Lord with all your heart...' (Proverbs 3:5).

It does not mean that by becoming a Christian we are somehow overnight made superhuman and are so confident in God's provision for our lives that we never need to have a care or worry ever again. Faith does not guarantee physical or material prosperity, as we continue to live in a damaged World into which the reality of God's Kingdom has only partially broken.

It does mean, however, that we have a Saviour who has experienced and understands the troubles of life that we face and who will walk alongside and support us through those troubles. And, ultimately, we have the unshakeable and unbreakable guarantee of salvation when our time on Earth is done.

God invites us all (metaphorically speaking) to walk on the water…are we ready to get our feet wet?

Bold

Too long have I lived with a surfeit of caution,
Content to let safety be my chosen portion,
Too often made worry my touchstone for living,
Forgetting that time can be short, unforgiving.
Though I'm too well aware there are other roads waiting,
The fear I might fail leaves me still hesitating
To swim to the deep, letting go of the side,
To go with the flow of a different tide.

It's all about courage that's anchored in trust,
If I'm ever to change, this is really a must:
To practise the things I'm too ready to preach,
To show it by action as well as in speech.
My boldness awakened, to follow His leading,
With fear put aside, so much old ground conceding,
As I look to His plan for my living unmasking,
'If not now, tell me when?' is a question worth asking.

My failure to act must be put to the sword,
For if there's no risk, there can be no reward;
I should be stepping out in a way that is new,
Taking courage to push long held barriers through.
If I truly believe that the Lord's on my side,
I must lower the drawbridge, and no longer hide
Behind high defences; I won't need to cower,
Pressing on my advance, wielding salvation's power.

The chains of the past are beginning to chafe
At the thought of my once again playing it safe;
Yet great mountains are shattered to fragmented boulders
When I'm lifted up high onto His broader shoulders.
When my caution is thrown to the strong wind that's blowing,
That is when I can reach for His Spirit full growing;
It is then I'll be ready to follow His leading,
My loss turned to gain that will see me succeeding.

It is mine to surrender, a will that's uncertain,
To let in the light, to draw back the dark curtain,
Embracing the fullness that He has to give,
With a faith that is driven by boldness to live;
Without fear of failing, knowing deep in my heart
That He's rooting for me and will never depart.

What do I have to fear, how can doubt have a place,
When He holds me secure by His love and His grace?
Let me stand up, be counted, my destiny meet,
Consigning anxiety to certain defeat;
To achieve so much more, when I choose to be bold:
Then, at last, I might see a full future unfold.

Fully Known

By God I am completely known, He's loved me from the start,
But just how fully can I say I'm giving Him my heart?
My fervour too soon left to fade, the flower still not blooming,
Distracted by the World's allure, too eagerly consuming.

For though He daily reaches out, I often miss my cue,
By acting on a different stage, forsake His sure review;
Instead of walking by His side, I simply pass Him by,
Yet find the road I've chosen is deserted, arid, dry.

Though He is everything I need, from all my darkness, pardon,
My heart remains for me to give, or hold it closed, to harden;
If I don't seek Him as I should, too soon He sees straight through me,
And, but for grace, He could have said: 'you never really knew me'.

Although I have the failings of a weak and feeble man,
I long to draw Him closer, in whatever way I can;
While I can only see in part from this side of the veil,
I pray for strength that my devotion won't be left to pale;
That when at last He calls me back, my faith will be full grown,
In Heaven, Him to fully know, as I am fully known.

Too Big an Ask?

It seems there are things far too hard to discuss:
Like believing in something that's greater than us,
Instilling a fear of our losing control,
This just isn't a rock that we're willing to roll;
When all preconceptions are taken to task,
The choice to believe is just too big an ask.

Assuming our needs are so easily met
Is a view so ingrained that it can't be upset;
Our plan for the battle we're keeping alive,
Though we know from first contact it cannot survive;
Too easy to make cool indifference a mask,
When to choose to believe feels like too much to ask.

Convinced our own truth will be setting us free,
Our comfort is found in the things we can see;
With our vision restricted to self-enclosed space,
There is nothing that's new, and no dreams to be chased;
In our self-satisfaction, content, still, to bask,
When believing in God is too much of an ask.

Is it simply the question we don't understand?
For if everything's held in the palm of His hand,
And if all that we need has been offered for free
When we open our heart, just how hard can it be?
With our future secured, and not out on a limb:
Is it too big an ask, our believing in Him?

Confident

No matter our trust may seem feeble and small,
God loves that we seek Him and answer His call;
The depth of our faith He's not looking to measure:
It's in our believing we give Him true treasure.

Knowing that all has been formed by His will,
That the spaces between He is ready to fill,
That a time fast approaches when none can ignore Him,
When all becomes clear as the World kneels before Him,
We take comfort our future in Jesus is sealed:
The Lord our protector, with faith as our shield.

A faith that is confident, steady and sure,
That stands firm with time and will always endure;
Assured by the promise of what is unseen,
That isn't here yet, but has forever been;
His Word is the anchor and Jesus the sign,
That our stars in the heavens will surely align;
Holding fast to our faith, we receive our reward:
A glorious future spent praising the Lord.

Walking on the Water (a song)

I never heard You speak in far-off days and distant lands,
Or felt the cruel marks they made upon your feet and hands;
I never shared the first cup that was only filled with tears,
Yet still I know You've been with me across so many years.

I didn't know the blind and lame that You had come to save,
I wasn't there when Lazarus was rescued from the grave;
I didn't taste the water that You turned to wedding wine,
And yet I drink the cup my Saviour fills with love divine:

Chorus
I'm walking on the water in my heart,
So glad with You I've made a brand new start,
And I pray from You I'll never be apart:
For I believe in You,
and all that You do.

I wasn't at Golgotha when the victory was won,
When all my sin was heaped upon the Father's only Son;
I wasn't in the temple, I didn't see the curtain torn,
When You died for me in anguish 'midst the mocking and the scorn.

I wasn't at the graveside when the stone was rolled away,
I missed the resurrection on that glorious Easter Day;
I didn't have the chance to touch the hands that Thomas saw,
And yet I know You died, and rose; that You will come once more:

Chorus

Day by day I'm walking where I've never walked before,
The wonders of your love and grace to fill me more and more;
Day by day I'm walking where I've never walked before,
The wonders of your love and grace to fill me more and more:

Chorus

I believe in You, and all that You do.

SONGS OF FORGIVENESS

Bear with each other and forgive whatever grievances you may have against one another. Forgive as the Lord forgave you.

Colossians 3:13

The forgiver and the forgiven

Harbouring unforgiveness and resentment is like deliberately and constantly picking open a festering wound: it harms us far more than the person from whom we withhold forgiveness.

Sometimes the hardest thing can be to recognise our own need for forgiveness; and it can be just as hard to accept it when it is offered to us. But it is only when we do so, that we will be able to let go of the many hurts and resentments (real or perceived) that we keep stored up, and allow ourselves to embrace the freedom and release that comes from forgiving others.

Jesus' forgiveness for our sins was a once and for all forgiveness, achieved for us by his dying in our place on the Cross. It does not need repeating; it covers not only the sin of our past, but also our sins today and those of our future.

We do still need to keep coming back to Jesus to seek his forgiveness when our thoughts, attitudes and actions fall short of how he calls us to live.

We do not do this to assure our salvation – that has already been secured at the point at which we accepted him as our personal Saviour.

We come to him to acknowledge our need for his ongoing mercy and grace, as he daily picks us up when we fall, takes us by the hand, and gently steers us back towards something that is so much better.

Forgiveness

Forgiveness brings peace and contentment,
Forgiving brings calm to the soul;
To put aside clinging resentment,
Gently cleansing, a balm making whole.

When we recognise we have been pardoned,
Yet not because it has been earned,
When He softens our hearts that were hardened,
True forbearance is no longer spurned.

Thanking Jesus for grace freely granted,
As we kneel at the sound of His name,
In our hearts feel His truth deeply planted,
That in love He bore all of our shame.

As we hear the kind words that are spoken,
One by one our tough layers He's peeling,
Then, at last, we may see our pride broken
And the way to bless others revealing.

There is truly no greater releasing
Than forgiving, like Him, in full measure;
To seek others' restoring, unceasing,
Is His gift, and the greatest of treasure.

Forgiveness Unforgotten

We talk about forgiveness as if it's just a word,
Maybe it is something that too often we have heard?
Becoming so familiar, we see its meaning lost,
Failing to remember just how much forgiveness cost.

God is perfect justice, but His mercy pushes through,
We should not lose sight of what our Saviour chose to do;
We ought to be remembering and thinking more than twice,
The freedom that He offers was secured at such a price.

Words can come so cheaply, but our actions speak more loudly:
To put aside the self-esteem to which we cling so proudly,
Assuming the humility He carried on the Cross
Will lead us to His saving grace that covers all our loss.

Laying at the core of all that Jesus came to win,
He leads us to redemption with forgiveness flooding in;
The depth of all it means should be forever in our hearts:
Embracing true forgiveness is when transformation starts.

Forgiveness Outspoken

When the World seeks a god in its own image made
We should aim to pour rain on the empty parade;
But it's not ours to judge, it is always God's call,
Remembering it's pride that precedes every fall.

'There's no smoke without fire', or so we are told,
But we shouldn't accept all the lies that we're sold;
We should not judge a book by its cover alone,
With the page left unturned and the content unknown.

Though possession may be some nine tenths of the law,
What we hope to acquire will still leave us poor;
Repentance at leisure's too bitterly faced,
When we seek to condemn, having acted in haste.

Turning in on ourselves leaves us no place to hide
When we seek retribution that flows from our pride;
We cannot seek a justice that's based on a whim,
No two wrongs make a right, we must leave it to Him.

Time is a great healer, so now is the time
For us not to return to the scene of the crime;
Sweet sorrow's departing, free given by grace,
Calling us to move on, leaves forgiveness in place.

To reject condemnation should be more than token,
We must more than speak out, we should be so outspoken
That we won't be content to let sleeping dogs lie,
If the tail wags the dog, we should ask ourselves why.

Angels hold back where the fool rushes in,
Now the slate must be wiped clean of every sin,
Recognising in all there is something that's good,
For all will be well, if we do as He would.

To believe in our heart and confess in our saying
Should be the foundation of all of our praying;
When the Lord sets the tone in a manner of speaking,
His grace is enough; it is always worth seeking.

SONGS OF GRACE

…God raised us up with Christ and seated us with him in the heavenly realms in Christ Jesus, in order that in the coming ages he might show the incomparable riches of his grace, expressed in his kindness to us in Christ Jesus. For it is by grace you have been saved, through faith – and this not from yourselves, it is the gift of God…

Ephesians 2:6-8

The greatest gift

What do we mean when we talk about God's grace?

It means that we can receive, without cost to ourselves, every good thing that God has to offer, because he freely gave his all for us. We are made spiritually rich, beyond measure, by his impoverishing himself through the selfless sacrifice of his only Son upon the Cross.

He died in our place (paying the price for all our wrongs), so that we might inherit eternal life – which is the greatest gift of all.

For all that we might try, we cannot make ourselves good enough for Heaven. We have all sinned and we all 'fall short of the glory of God' (Romans 3:23). It is precisely for this reason that we need Jesus, who is without sin, to stand in our place and take the punishment we deserve, so that God's righteous judgment against us is fully satisfied. The awesome sacrifice made by Jesus in bearing the burden of all of our sins frees us from a debt that is beyond our ability to pay.

We have all been given the opportunity to be the recipients of the most extraordinary, and yet undeserved, reward. We should not let it slip from our grasp. All we have to do is say yes.

Mercy and Grace

There's no gradient of sin,
We're all treated the same;
It is not for the well,
But the sick, that He came.
God's love far outshines ours,
And puts in the shade
The faltering steps towards
Mercy we've made.

When we set ourselves up
To apportion the blame,
To condemn others' sin,
As if we're not the same;
If we make ourselves judges,
Forgiveness refused,
Denying the truth
That we, too, are accused;
We give in to resentment,
Reluctant to face
That our hearts won't acknowledge
God's mercy and grace.

Then we show just how loveless
Ours souls have become:
Though He gives the bread to us,
There's barely a crumb
That to those undeserving
We're willing to share;
That they should be forgiven
It seems so unfair;
Still, we're blind to the truth
That we're in the same place:
For we, too, have been saved
By God's mercy and grace.

It's for us to be searching
The depths of our heart,
For it is only then
True repentance can start;
There's no greater or lesser,
We've all fallen short,
It is only through Christ
That our future is bought.
We must all stand as one,
And together embrace
The incredible truth of
God's mercy and grace.

Undeserved

Just when it seems we are wholly defeated,
With all we hold dear deeply cursed;
When all thoughts of goodness have long since retreated,
The trail of our loss is reversed.

So much consumed, and yet still undernourished,
With all that's still left on our plate;
A slate that is marred, we can never wipe cleaner,
That seems an immovable weight.

Light out of darkness, a crevice appearing,
A glimpse of the Sun breaking through;
After so long entrenched, heavy mired in our failings,
God steers us to something so new.

He leads us to winning, when our ways are losing,
To stand at the head of the line;
Brings our bitterest cup to a place of such sweetness,
Turns our water to rich wedding wine.

For once we no longer pursue empty rainbows,
And seek Him instead with our prayer,
Surrendered to Him, He brings promised salvation,
Our every burden to bear.

He finds us and lifts us, when we're at rock bottom,
From the foot to the top of the curve,
The triumph of mercy that saves us from judgment,
So much more than we ever deserve.

Every day, we should come on our knees to the Father,
Deeply humbled by all that He's done;
Though we've nothing to bring, we've the greatest of gifts,
With new life by the grace of the Son!

Given by Grace

How marvellous this gift of grace;
When Jesus died to take our place,
With heavy barbs so cruelly driven,
A sinless life was freely given,
Surrendered on a Cross of wood,
Defeating fear of death for good.

Though, for a moment, all seemed lost,
His rising showed He'd paid the cost;
He cast aside the pall of gloom,
Emerged, victorious, from the tomb.

With nail-pierced hands flung open wide
The power of God now undenied,
His sharing gifts, no holding back,
In boundless love, no favours lack;
And by His grace, turned inside out,
Our lives set free from chains of doubt;
His endless mercy sets us free,
Becoming who we're made to be.

And every gift that we receive,
Another Heaven-sent reprieve
From all the trials in this place,
Before we meet Him, face to face.
His Kingdom, though yet seen in part
Shines in upon each longing heart;
It's ours the joy to freely share,
To lead the lost to greet Him there:
The time which all Creation yearns,
That glorious day, when He returns!

Endless Grace

Jesus casts aside the sin that mars our daily living;
If we confess, with humble heart, our all He'll be forgiving.
But though He lifts us to our feet, we cannot help but stumble;
Our will to stand, and not to fall, too soon can quickly crumble.

Though He has conquered once, for all, removing empty yearning,
We still must seek His face each day, and never stop returning.
He satisfies our hungry hearts, His Spirit is the leaven;
But all remains to be fulfilled while still this side of Heaven.

So we must come before His throne, surrendered adoration
Should be our constant offering; to long for transformation.
One prayer will never be enough, there has to be repeating,
Contrite for all we're falling short: the power of sin unseating.

Forgiveness, like an endless stream that washes us, unceasing;
Our every seam that's out of place is straightened, without creasing.
For us, salvation, made secure, by Jesus' death and rising:
Let's worship Him for all He gives, His grace and mercy prizing!

SONGS OF HUMILITY

…whoever exalts himself will be humbled, and whoever humbles himself will be exalted.

Matthew 23:12

Do not think of yourself more highly than you ought, but rather think of yourself with sober judgment, in accordance with the measure of faith God has given you.

Romans 12:3

Looking to others

It is said that 'pride goes before destruction, a haughty spirit before a fall' (Proverbs 16:18).

How often are we so proud of our own accomplishments, only to see our handiwork diminished or reduced to little or nothing, by circumstances or events beyond our control? How often do we build ourselves up in our minds, blind to our own shortcomings and limitations, only to discover that we are not so great after all?

Surely there has never been anyone with more cause for pride in himself than Jesus, God's only perfect, sinless, Son: yet he made himself a servant of all and in an act of ultimate humility freely chose to exchange his power and glory for humiliation and a cruel death, for the sake of us all; for you and me.

Should we not take a leaf out of the book of the greatest person ever to walk the Earth, and try, as best we can, to reorient our perspective away from ourselves, ready and willing instead to give humble service for the good of others?

Let us not take pride in who we are (or think we are), but rather recognise our true state, and give humble gratitude for the unconditional acceptance and love that God lavishes upon us.

Beginner

Not much of a saint, but much more of a sinner,
In living out good I am just a beginner;
I have to start somewhere, if only I try,
Perhaps opportunities won't pass me by.

I am no expert, I've no special skill,
I'm only equipped by the power of God's will;
As I'm touched by the breath of His still, quiet voice,
To follow His prompting, He gives me the choice:
I can walk in His footsteps, or go my own way,
But when I let Him lead, I cannot go astray.

Though I'm one tiny voice in a glorious choir,
His praises will soar, with His name lifted higher;
When I give myself up, as His hands and His feet,
It is then He will bring Earth and Heaven to meet.

What do I have to offer, so little my own?
Yet by sowing His seed, mighty forests are grown;
Great mountains are moved at the wave of His hand,
And His every good purpose through Jesus will stand.

Though to live as He wills, I may only be starting,
Still, little by little, old ways are departing;
I can face any challenge, complete any race,
When transformed and empowered by God's mercy and grace.

More of You

I long to have much more of You,
Be here to stay, not passing through;
To hold on fast to all You give,
To make your love the place I live.

I want to have much less of me,
To find the one I'm made to be;
With hope, with gratitude and praise,
By faith to follow in your ways.

I want to see the bubble burst,
To lose my pride and put You first;
To seek a wholly new design,
New wineskin made to hold new wine.

I want to set a different trend,
Made whole from broken, fit to mend;
Pursuing You with full accord,
In You, my heart and soul restored.

I long to put myself aside,
My arms for You flung open wide:
Your goodness, Lord, to see me through:
With less of me, and more of You.

Captive Hearts

The choice is ours to follow Him, submission offered free,
A willing, given, service, as in faith we bend the knee;
No longer chained as slaves to sin, but servants of the Lord,
When freely all we have is given of our own accord.

We only really flourish when our need we recognise;
The truth is laid before us, but we have to claim the prize:
By giving us His everything, He looks for nothing less,
When we decide to give our all, then He will truly bless.

It must be all or nothing, but the choice is ours to make:
Accept the sacrifice He made in dying for our sake,
The fullness of His grace is ours to honour and to treasure,
We're called to seek Him heart and soul, there can be no half measure.
His Spirit living in us leads to perfect liberty;
It's only when we've captive hearts that we are truly free.

Where Angels Fear to Tread

They told us, from our earliest years,
That life is what we choose to make;
That nothing lost is nothing gained,
But everything is ours to take.
They told us that it's up to us,
That all control is ours to choose,
We have it all within ourselves,
That, being bold, we'll never lose.

They told us that we must rely
On our own, certain, inner voice;
That we alone have what it takes
For understanding every choice.
They told us just to plough ahead,
By our own wisdom so empowered,
With nothing more for our success,
The taste of victory never soured.

Yet as our webs, so smartly spun,
Begin to tear and fall away,
With all direction we once had
Gone south, no longer holding sway;
When all our schemes are in the wind,
So many dreams blown into dust,
No longer with the same allure,
A shine that fades, and turns to rust;
It's only then we start to see
The World is not in our control;
There's only One who keeps us safe,
To cherish every longing soul.

If we had walked a different road,
Not thinking of ourselves as kings;
If we had found humility,
The path to truly precious things;
If we had recognised the One
Who holds our future in His hand,
And sought the wisdom that His Word
Alone can help us understand;
If hollow crowns were cast aside,
Perhaps we might have sooner found
It's only putting trust in God
That leads us onto higher ground.

They told us all we wished to hear,
We thought that this would make us whole;
The danger fully overlooked:
To gain the World, but lose the soul.
Perhaps we should have exercised
A little common sense, instead:
Did no one tell us fools rush in,
In places angels fear to tread?

Songs of Mercy

The Lord is not slow in keeping his promise, as some understand slowness. He is patient with you, not wanting anyone to perish, but everyone to come to repentance.

2 Peter 3:9

Putting things right

Many people doubt the goodness of God and question how a caring and loving God can allow all the pain and suffering that we see in the World. Why doesn't he do something about it?

The answer is: he has! In the greatest act of self-sacrifice the World has ever known, God himself in the person of his Son has given his very life to defeat the power of sin and death, opening the way for all who believe to pass from their broken state into a completely blessed and restored existence.

But even accepting that truth, why did he wait so long to act and why, two millennia later, are we still stuck in this damaged and pain-filled World, waiting for God to finish what he started?

The truth is that God is not slow to act.

God operates outside of our time-limited linear existence. In the eternal scheme of things, the entire history of mankind can be seen as less than the blink of an eye, or as a single grain of sand in a vast desert.

We might think of it like this: it's as if the World came into being this morning, Jesus' death and resurrection took place at lunchtime and his Second Coming will occur later this evening. In that sense, just a few short hours have passed since Creation started, and there remain just a few more hours for everyone to make up their minds about God.

God did not have to wait for us at all. It is only because of his great compassion and mercy that he has held back for so long the judgment that we all deserve. That he gives us this extra time is because, out of his great love, he longs for us to turn back to him and accept the amazing gift of forgiveness and redemption that he freely offers.

But will we choose to accept?

Slow

Sometimes, when everything is going wrong,
We wonder why He's waited for so long
To lift us from the darkness and the dirt,
To put aside the aching and the hurt.
Still others say that if He really cared,
From centuries of longing we'd be spared,
That in an instant we'd be turned around
And lifted from the mire to holy ground.

But He is not as slow as some might think,
For we are ever standing on the brink:
If not today, the hour is coming soon
When there's no longer time to change our tune;
The home we seek is not a distant dream,
The end is not as far as it may seem;
In Heaven's timing, only moments stand
Before deliverance to the promised land.

Although sometimes it may be hard to see,
Creation turns the way it's meant to be;
To fret about the time, we should be slow,
Assured that God is always in the know.
It's He alone decides the time and place
When there will be an end to this short race;
The age-long promises all broken through,
The old being replaced by wondrous new.

For now, we walk along the very edge,
Between the now and then, a narrow ledge,
At any moment called to cross the line,
Exchanging all we've known for the divine.

He is not slow to act, as some suppose,
But, reaching out in love to each of those
Yet to respond, to give a final chance
To change their steps, pursue a different dance,
To see things in a wholly altered light,
Inviting God to come and make things right.

And so, the clock is surely ticking down,
The day will soon be ours to claim the crown
That we are freely offered if we choose:
With Jesus on our side, we cannot lose;
His love for us can never be denied,
We couldn't be raised higher if we tried.

To this great promise we keep holding fast:
Though seeming long, the wait is in the past;
For everything is to the second planned,
Our future held securely by His hand.

A Simple Man

How is it I, a simple man,
Stand centre stage in this great plan?
So undeserving of reward,
Receiving what I scarce afford.
Beyond all means of wealth, of heart,
My debt is covered from the start;
Though to the World, it all seems lost,
He makes the way and pays the cost.
So bittersweet, the bread and wine,
Points to an end that should be mine.

So, comes the day, we lift Him high,
Deserted, scorned and left to die;
And we are given front-row seats
To share this cruellest of defeats;
Or so it seems, for all the world,
His purposes as yet unfurled.
Unknowing, that from ghastly loss
Salvation rises from the Cross;
A World that sees a broken man,
Yet blinded to the greater plan.

Though to the World, it makes no sense,
I see a future far from tense;
The curtain torn, I stand and wait,
His promises to contemplate.
Though to the World, it seems absurd,
Content, I take Him at His word.
The sting is drawn, the healing done,
He claims the prize, the race is run;
Such hope cannot be left to die,
The third day comes, He's lifted high.

How is it I, a simple man,
Am saved before the World began?
This matchless love, I stand in awe,
To worship Him for evermore.

One God

There is no fighting to be done,
The battle is already won;
No other occupies His throne:
There is One God, and Him alone.

Unconfined by time and space,
His power prevails in every place;
His holy presence knows no bounds,
The skies are full of Heaven's sounds.

For He is One, and One in all,
He stands while all around Him fall;
Omnipotent, His reach complete:
All challengers face sure defeat.

The other gods we choose to seek
Have naught to say and cannot speak,
Existing only in our minds,
A fragile tie that never binds.

Our idols must be set aside,
An end to self and foolish pride;
For He alone can raise us up,
And take away our bitter cup
That, without Him, we surely face:
Restoring us by love and grace.

Though righteous judgment offers grief,
His mercy, still, can bring relief;
Accepting Jesus as our Lord,
He pays the cost we can't afford;
No longer by our sin enslaved:
In true submission, we are saved.

By Jesus' blood, we have been freed,
There is no other that we need;
Of everything, the cornerstone:
One God, and only Him alone.

SONGS OF SACRIFICE

...if anybody does sin, we have one who speaks to the Father in our defence – Jesus Christ, the Righteous One. He is the atoning sacrifice for our sins, and not only for ours but also for the sins of the whole world.

1 John 2:1-2

Perfect surrender

God is a God of justice, but he is also a God of love and mercy. Not wanting anyone to perish, he sent his one and only Son to inhabit a frail mortal body just like ours, to share with us the experience of both the joy and the pain of life and, ultimately, to submit to a brutal and agonising death.

In an act of the greatest self-sacrifice ever known, the perfect man surrendered himself and gave up his life in the knowledge that only that sacrifice would be sufficient to satisfy God's righteous judgment for all the wrongs that we have done.

In doing so, he secured for all who accept him as Saviour the wonders of eternal life with God.

This was no easy ride: but trust in God enabled him to face the extreme darkness of the storm that swirled around him that first Easter, and to emerge victorious in the calm of a glorious resurrection morning.

Moved

Stars aren't supposed to move, but this One did;
From Heaven, this a bold, audacious, bid:
To choose to make an entry in this way,
God brought His very person into play.

Kings don't give up their thrones, but this One chose
To be a common man, with body blows;
Determined, for a time, to be the same
As each and every soul for whom He came.

The highest don't descend, but this One fell,
Though of His own accord, He knew too well
His coming down would see Him lifted high:
But not exalted, raised instead to die.

The strongest don't concede, but this One gave
Up all He had, surrendered to the grave;
For only through His weakness could be found
The power to lead us back to higher ground.

The rich don't sell it all, but this One paid
His everything, a new foundation laid;
With none held back, of His whole self He shared:
The depth of giving showed how much He cared.

Stars aren't supposed to move, but this One rose,
And, through His light, redemption power flows;
His sacrifice delivers life and peace,
Eternal wonder that will never cease!

Before the Calm

So, this is how the end began:
Untrustworthy, the whims of man,
Cold hate replacing praises warm,
That pointed to a coming storm.
For though they raised Him up on high,
It was to let them see Him die,
Condemned, into a place of harm,
The gathering storm before the calm.

Although it seemed the line was crossed,
That all the hope He brought was lost,
Yet, this the moment, to begin
His victory, disarming sin;
To finish what He came to do
The door flung wide, for me and you:
He bore the load through nail-pierced palm,
To ride the storm before the calm.

At three, deep darkness stalked the land,
The Sun withdrawn by Heaven's hand,
The curtain torn from top to tail,
The great divide could not prevail;
For from this ending, He would win
The start of new life, ushered in.
He reached to us with outstretched arm:
Embraced the storm before the calm.

Three days gone past, removed the stone,
He lives, to make the saved His own,
With all the turmoil of the past
Consigned into the ground, at last.
The light of resurrection day
Has swept the sting of death away,
The World, remade in different form:
His calm, that overcame the storm.

The Price

When we were lost and far away,
God would not let the dark hold sway;
Though we had nothing we could give,
He paid the price, that we might live.

So cruelly tortured, soul and mind,
There was no solace He could find,
With all our fault in Him subsumed,
A crushing isolation loomed.

More than His body to forsake,
He felt as if His heart would break:
The hardest thing for Him to bear,
His Father seemed no longer there.

But with this strange transaction done,
In Him He made us each God's Son,
Where justice and His mercy met,
Our souls were saved, our future set.

Love kept Him on that cruel Cross,
Accepting He must take the loss;
The only way to clear our sins:
Death's power ends, new life begins.

Surrendering to poverty,
He gave His all to set us free;
His sacrifice made in our place
Buys us the riches of His grace.

Another Nail

If I let my faith grow cold,
When within myself I fold,
Self-importance taking hold;
When I've given in to sin,
Glorying in empty pride,
I cause the truth to be denied.
See, His arms are open wide:
Another nail is driven in.

When I'm lost, He's always there
To shoulder an uneven share,
How quickly I forget His care:
That He should be forever praised.
How often I ignore the price,
And act as if His sacrifice
Was, for the moment, put on ice:
Again, I see the hammer raised.

When I'm treading on the rest,
So that I can be 'the best',
I completely fail the test
Of who my Lord would have me be;
When my want becomes my need,
Imprisoning me by my greed,
The only way that I'll be freed
Is by His hanging on the tree.

Every time my guard is down,
Seeking for myself the crown,
Instead of singing His renown,
Again, they pierce His fragile hand.
And so, once more, I put on ice
His one eternal sacrifice,
As if there never was a price:
Yet this is what the Father planned.

Sometimes, for the truth I reach,
But seem to lose the power of speech,
Forsaking all He came to teach:
Afraid I might be called to stand –
Then, instead of walking proud,
Declaring the Lord's praises loud,
I lose myself among the crowd:
As if the hammer's in my hand.

When my fault I fail to see,
Blaming anyone but me,
Once more, He hangs upon the tree:
The nails are given deadly play;
I act as if His sacrifice
Had, once again, been put on ice,
Denying that he paid the price:
In ignorance, content to stay.

When the call to life I shun,
When I simply turn and run
From the good I might have done:
Then, I leave Him, hanging there,
Languishing upon the tree,
Crying for our misery:
'Why have you forsaken me?'
To pay the cost we cannot bear.

Turned away, my eyes remain
Shielded from my Saviour's pain,
Denying all He died to gain:
I take, instead, the easy road.
In my mind, His sacrifice
Disappears like melting ice,
Forgetting I would pay the price,
Without His precious blood that flowed.

Yet, as the nails are hammered in
To crush, in shame, the power of sin,
To understand, I can't begin,
This victory, from strange defeat.
Though the World would see Him fail,
By the power of tree and nail,
Over all He will prevail,
Enthroned upon the judgement seat.

And still, today, His life to give
In agony, that I might live;
His body piercing like a sieve
That sifts again my every sin.
Although two thousand years have passed,
For me, He still is holding fast;
Today, once more, He breathes His last:
Another nail is driven in.

SONGS OF THANKSGIVING

Enter his gates with thanksgiving and his courts with praise; give thanks to him and praise his name. For the Lord is good and his love endures for ever; his faithfulness continues through all generations.

Psalm 100:4-5

More than enough

In a World of plenty, how is it that what we never seem to have enough?

For all that we possess, why does an envy of those who have more than us still persist and leave us forever unsatisfied?

No matter the extent of our wealth and our possessions, we fail to count our blessings and instead remain unthankful for the abundance that we have, determined not to rest until we have filled our coffers to the brim. We somehow fool ourselves that it is in all this striving for more that true contentment will be found.

However, for so many, the reality that eventually dawns is that all of this accumulation is like dust in the wind, here one moment and blown away the next.

True and everlasting security comes only from the One who holds our future, and that of all Creation, in his hands. God's saving grace is of value beyond measure.

The extraordinary truth is that all that we will ever need for the most complete and perfectly fulfilled eternal existence is offered to us by God, freely, and without cost on our part.

Our heart and soul should do nothing less than overflow with gratitude and thanksgiving for the loving Saviour who spends his all to give us everything.

And our thankfulness for all that Jesus has done for us should find its natural expression through abundant and unrestrained worship and praise. Hallelujah!

Credit

We think we're so hard done by, bigger picture rarely seeing,
Our sense that we're downtrodden becomes a state of being;
We feel ourselves impoverished, our purses getting lighter:
Yet, pound for pound, we are the very richest sort of fighter.

Though blessed with rising credit, we're still acting like a debtor;
We think we have so little, and that others do much better,
When of our many blessings we should not be losing count:
In truth, we have a fortune of an infinite amount.

For all we see as valuable, as worthy of our trust,
Too quickly fades to nothing and lies trampled in the dust;
The sum of the possessions that we seek to pile much higher
Are nothing more than kindling for a coming funeral pyre.
We overlook the value of what stares us in the face,
A benefit so priceless, that no money could replace;
The greatest of all purchases, that we cannot afford,
Is given to us freely through the mercy of the Lord.

In for a penny, for a pound, He empties every coffer,
The riches that He offers us, there is no greater offer;
A place that is not ours to earn with any sum of money:
The home that Jesus promises will flow with milk and honey.

The currency of Heaven turns our losses into gains,
Without a farthing spent by us, our perfect end ordains;
With Him there's only profit, every loss is cancelled out:
Full payment for redemption, there has never been a doubt;
The balance in our favour, no more shortfall, profit mounts:
The glory of our Saviour gives the greatest of accounts!

Blessings

I find it hard to contemplate where I would be right now
If all the blessings I'd received were left to take a bow;
If I had never known His love that simply could not fail,
If I had tried to trust in my own efforts to prevail.
But by His grace in reaching out, He offered something true,
That promised to outshine what I alone might try to do.
Yet in my deepest dreaming, still, I never could have guessed
That things would surely come to this: how fully I'd be blessed.

I didn't have to make the mark, He wasn't keeping score,
For as I looked to Him in faith my blessings blossomed more;
He showed me all I had to do was follow what I'd heard,
To reap the harvest of His grace, by trusting in His Word;
Yet, in my deepest hoping, still, I never would have dared
To contemplate the blessings that my Saviour freely shared.

My every waking moment calls for gratitude outpoured,
I cannot find the words enough to glorify my Lord;
I can but praise Him every day for all that He has done:
The greatest blessing of them all is found in God's own Son.

To meet my deepest hopes and dreams my God will never rest,
He gives me all the good I have: by Him I'm truly blessed!

Never Stop

Let's never stop, for we should give Him praise, our praise forever,
Our sure connection to the Lord, there's nothing that can sever.
Let's never stop our thankfulness, so much that we are gifted,
Let's never stop our songs of praise, with every voice uplifted;
And never stop exalting Him, to give Him all the glory,
For He has written every word of our eternal story.

Let's never stop our wonderment, our sense of awe, elation
For all that He has done for us, delivering salvation;
Let's never stop expressing love, for He has loved us greater,
He holds our souls within His hands, our glorious Creator.

Let's never stop rejoicing, there's so much worth celebrating,
With so much more that's still to come, our souls anticipating;
Let's never stop our eagerness to find our place of resting,
When all the hope we have in Him is gloriously cresting.

Let's never stop our songs, our praise, our wonder, our elating,
Secure that all His promises are truly worth the waiting;
And when we think that we have given all we have in store,
Let's raise our voices, start again, and praise Him all the more!

SONGS FOR A TIME YET TO COME
PART 5: THE LOVING GOD

SONGS OF COMMUNITY

May the grace of the Lord Jesus Christ, and the love of God, and the fellowship of the Holy Spirit be with you all.

2 Corinthians 13:14

...let us consider how we may spur one another on towards love and good deeds. Let us not give up meeting together, as some are in the habit of doing, but let us encourage one another – and all the more as you see the Day approaching.

Hebrews 10:24-25

United as one

God is a relational God and, being made in his image, we too are naturally relational creatures.

The Church is all about relationships: our own personal relationship with Jesus; our corporate relationship as the body of Christ; and our relationship with the Created Order. We are many and so different and yet we are also one common people, children of God, joined together in faith; individually diverse and yet at our core one and the same.

We crave and actively seek connection with others, most powerfully driven by our capacity and longing for love. We are made not to be independent but interdependent people.

In God, this is most keenly demonstrated in the Trinity: that we worship a God who, in a mysterious sense, is 'three in one': three persons who are at the same time inseparable as one.

This is key to understanding who God really is, but it is a baffling concept to get our heads around. But God does not expect us to understand everything about him; nor are we capable of doing so. The important thing is to trust that God reveals all that we need to know about him for now, as we look forward, in faith, to the glorious future that he has planned for us.

One of the many examples that has been used to try to explain the concept of the Trinity (albeit in simple terms) is this: to his children, a man is a father; to his parents, he is a son; and to his wife, he is a husband. In each case, relationally different, but all still the one man: they represent three different aspects of the same person.

And we have the exciting prospect of joining and fully experiencing that amazing family relationship with God, when he finally calls us home to be with him.

In today's self-absorbed World, it is too easy to let ourselves become resigned to the prospect of a future pointing only to a World of diminishing faith, where any connection to God is fading fast. And yet, although it may often feel like a sense of real community is in decline, God has not given up on us. He still longs to draw us to himself, bound together in unity and love.

Decline

We see the decline of once great institutions,
No longer relied on to offer solutions;
What once was revered, now so often untrusted,
With all we thought solid so easily busted.

We're viewing the World through a permanent frown,
With no one to look up to, we only look down;
No longer think once, now inclined to think twice
About those we had trusted to offer advice.

Taking a dive, we lose hope in our leaders,
Who have sunk from the top, to become bottom feeders;
The altar of self is not one they would die on,
Their motives so suspect, that none can rely on.

To whom can we turn when there is so much needing,
Where there's only mistrust that appears to be breeding?
There is One who knows all, long before it's begun,
If we look to His leading, through faith in His Son;
The wisdom of God is a solid foundation
On which to rebuild every people and nation.

Yet though many for God may still claim to be rooting,
It is only themselves in the foot they are shooting,
When the cellars they draw from have run short of wine,
As they see their one purpose to manage decline.
Resigned to the thought no one's paying attention,
They think speaking His name isn't worthy of mention;
That no one is listening, there is no relief,
For a World turned from God, wholly lacking belief.

So those we should look to for making a stand,
To open a path to a different land,
Instead, losing sight of the aces they're holding,
Leave them unplayed, with a winning hand folding.
They are closed to the truth, and so sorely mistaken,
For surrendering isn't the road to be taken:
The World runs its course, but our God's never finished,
His power sustained, it remains undiminished.

To lift us to heights so much greater than ever,
Our connection to Him there is none that can sever;
Though the waves toss and turn, and it's far from plain sailing,
We are resting assured God will never be failing.

We must not let the darkness become the defining
Of who we can be; God is never declining;
Though from all that He stands for, the World is estranging,
The Lord is eternal, forever unchanging.

Church

What is the Church? What does it mean in saying we belong?
Is it just a place where faithful masses love to throng,
A place to stand and look above, beyond each soaring spire;
Or could it be there's something more than structures to admire?

It's so much more than bricks and mortar, choir stalls and pews,
More than fonts of holy water, stained-glass window hues;
It's more than ancient words recited, filling empty spaces,
More than songs, familiar tunes, though all still have their places.

It's all about community, each sister and each brother,
Held together, sure in faith, in tune with one another;
Committed to a common cause, in praise and worship giving,
Standing far out from the crowd, a different way of living.

It's built around relationships, forged by our love for Jesus;
Beyond the fractious noise outside, His boundless mercy frees us,
To make in us one heart, one mind, set on the same agenda,
Called into service for the Lord, to be His great befriender,
To share the love bestowed on us, that all may yet inherit
An entry to the promised land, much more than we could merit.

Houses built on sand are to the water quickly blown,
For all that Jesus gives rests on a different cornerstone;
His Church is every one of us, the sum of many parts,
His grace the sure foundation that we carry in our hearts.

Three

The Holy Spirit, Father, Son,
Three persons that exist as one;
United love that lets us see
A perfect triune harmony.

Three sides that occupy one coin,
Unseparated by the join,
Reflect the richness of His grace,
We see in Him each different face.

In one sense they are all the same
And occupy a single frame;
All speaking with the one true mind,
Their separate parts do not unwind.

Though, in another way, they're more:
Three rooms to enter through one door;
But all connected, interlinked,
Each of their own, yet indistinct.

The Holy Spirit, Father, Son,
Three persons and yet only one;
A mystery of breathless awe
That presages what lies in store:
It's coming home that sets us free,
To join in His pure unity,
In every part to be related,
Brought in to be, as one, created.

SONGS OF CONNECTION

---

*[Jesus said] "A new command I give you: Love one another.
As I have loved you, so you must love one another."*

John 13:34

*Therefore encourage one another and build each other up, just
as in fact you are doing.*

1 Thessalonians 5:11

Subsumed into the machine

We live in an increasingly sophisticated technological World. It is a World of instant and incessant communication through a variety of electronic channels.

We have access to seemingly limitless information and knowledge at the click of a mouse. There is a myriad of opportunities for connecting with so many people in so many places, without our ever having to move an inch from where we are.

What wonders! What could possibly go wrong?

How is it that for all the benefits that modern technology seems to bring, we find ourselves ever less connected and ever more remote, in terms of real personal relationships?

Have we become just another unknown name on a list, another nameless face on a screen, another random number in a data sequence?

Are we content with so little, or might we instead seek real relationships, with real people, rather than accepting impersonal and distorted images on a screen?

This increasingly common tendency for weak ties, where interaction is remote, where relationships are held at arm's length, is like a metaphor for our modern condition, where so much of our existence is too easily reduced to the superficial and the impersonal.

But this is not how God made us to be. Jesus is the great connector: enabling us to connect with each other; with the World around us; and most importantly with God. He made us as mutually dependent people, with a need for close relationships, rather than for the solitary independence that the World so often seems to value.

In Jesus, we have the greatest example of someone who was perfectly and intimately connected to God; who trusted in his Heavenly Father for all his physical, emotional and spiritual needs; who was in a constant personal dialogue with God; and who enjoyed a depth of loving relationship far beyond the deepest of connections that we could ever imagine.

We were made to be connected. Real living is about making meaningful connection with others, be that in a first shared conversation with a new acquaintance; the nurturing of a deeper and more lasting friendship; or a meeting of two hearts that commits and endures for a lifetime.

Whoever we are and whatever our circumstances, nothing quite matches that sense of value and worth, of belonging and connection, that human relationships bring, particularly when we seek to live in communion with others in the ways that God intends for us.

In doing so, we can find ourselves drawn closer and ever more connected to him; and we may also be enabled to help others to do the same.

Disconnected

Some say we've never been connected more than we're now seeing,
In every aspect of our lives a very part of being
That we need never be alone, through calm and stormy weather,
Our lives forever intertwined, we'll always be together.

For science has created what has worked for us so purely,
Within a web so intricate, where we are held securely;
There's always someone we can call, our selves forever sharing,
Our hearts no longer on our sleeves, instead it's 'tech' we're wearing.

So much to see and yet we find relationships receding,
We drown in screen time overload while missing what we're needing.
Our keystrokes swim against the tide, where streams are ever flowing,
With many faces spend our time, but never truly knowing.

Some say there's always someone there, a click away from speaking,
And yet in our remoteness, we lose sight of what we're seeking.
The lines on which our links are drawn, our contacts intersected,
This virtual reality can leave us disconnected.

Though brought together instantly, the distances are looming,
Becoming ever digital, our very souls subsuming;
But still, might we yet put aside distraction that entices,
If someone pulled the plug and left us to our own devices?

Wrecked

The things we thought that should connect us,
Instead, in time, have only wrecked us;
It makes for such a poor relation,
When all we have is information.

And in the absence of real feeling,
Each precious moment, time is stealing;
As down the line, with aimless cruising,
We can't unlock the code we're using.

The station where we're daily waiting,
A bubble constantly deflating;
There's nothing real for us to see,
With all presented in 2D.

Too soon we're driven on the rocks,
No chance to make it to the docks,
When all we have are ones and noughts,
Unplugged from disconnected ports.

To live a life without the living
Will leave us cold and unforgiving;
And if we hide behind our screens,
Not knowing what that really means,
Those aimless keystrokes, left unchecked,
Will see us lost, and surely wrecked.

Connection

If we're to see relationships restored,
We need our own connection to the Lord;
In knowing Him, so others, too, can see
The way that God intends our lives to be.

In humble worship, the best place to start,
We have to reach for Him with all our heart;
To seek His goodness, mercy and His grace,
Our longing to meet Jesus face to face.

It's only when, by faith, we come to know
Who Jesus is, that blessings truly flow,
So we can shine, reflections of His love
Revealing waves of glory from above.

Such greater wonders we will see unfurled
By seeking to be Jesus to the World;
In drawing others closer to the Lord,
It's then that we receive our true reward.

It's all about connecting God to man,
Delivering the Father's perfect plan;
When we, obedient, humbly play our part,
It's then we'll see real transformation start.

SONGS OF INSIGHT

The Word became flesh and made his dwelling among us. We have seen his glory, the glory of the One and Only, who came from the Father, full of grace and truth.

John 1.14

Seeking His face

The awesome and unseeable glory of God is something referred to in number of places in the Bible.

In the Old Testament, we see the prophet Moses communing with God, as the people of Israel journey towards the Promised Land; and in response to a request from Moses to allow him to see God's glory, God replies 'I will cause all my goodness to pass in front of you... But ...you cannot see my face, for no-one may see me and live...' (Exodus 33:19-20).

And in the New Testament, the apostle Paul writes of the Lord '...who alone is immortal, and who lives in unapproachable light, whom no-one has seen or can see....' (1 Timothy 6:15-17).

So, how can we ever really understand or be sure about who God is, and what he is like?

If God were to show up today in all his power and glory, our fragile human bodies would simply be completely overwhelmed and blown away in an instant. It would be like finding ourselves standing five feet from the Sun – we would be instantly blinded by its light and immediately burnt up by its fire.

This is one of the key reasons why Jesus came to live among us as a man; so that we would be able to relate to him face to face, enabling us more fully to see and understand God's true nature.

So, while we cannot see God directly, in New Testament times we can know what God is like, from the character and life of Jesus (John 1:14). And although Jesus is no longer with us bodily, he has left us his Holy Spirit, who lives within all those who accept Jesus as their Saviour and through whom we can connect directly with God.

The Power and the Glory

You could have come with blazing fire, a warrior returned,
But we could not endure the heat, Creation would have burned;
Back then, our sinful selves still at the centre of the story:
We simply could not stand before your power and your glory.

You could have simply played it safe and stayed just where You were,
But love compelled You otherwise and caused your heart to stir;
Determined that all You had made should not be left to fail,
And knowing that, untended, broken nature would prevail,
You chose to lay down, for a time, your glory and your power,
To live among us as a man until your final hour.

You could have come with legions, armed with all of Heaven's might,
But You knew this would overwhelm our fragile human sight;
Your light outshining every Sun could only leave us blind,
And such an awesome majesty would simply blow our mind.
You chose, instead, the path of true humility and love,
Relying on the Spirit to connect to God above;
You showed us we could do the same, that soon would come the hour
When we could know You fully in your glory and your power.

You could have come in splendour, but it wasn't yet your time,
So much among us still to do, with mountains set to climb;
In your unfailing love for us, You walked the darkest road,
You carried all our burdens and You bore our heavy load.
You could have watched from Heaven, but the price You chose to pay,
A cruel Cross that beckoned, for there was no other way;
You could have turned away, and left us to our own devices,
Instead, You gave your life, the greatest of all sacrifices.

You could have simply given up and swept it all away,
Avoiding all the pain to come on crucifixion day;
But You resolved to make things right, to save and to restore,
Return us to the Father's heart, love centred at the core.

Now by your humbly stepping down from Heaven's lofty tower,
You've made a way for us to know the fullness of your power;
With eyes made new to gaze upon the everlasting star,
When You return, unveiled, we'll see You fully as You are!

Five Feet from the Sun

If we stood five feet from the Sun,
Our time on Earth would soon be done;
Its surging heat, its soaring power
Above our own so far would tower,
Our eyes could not maintain their sight,
Immersed in overwhelming light;
And, stood so close, completely burning,
We would to ashes be returning.

With God and us, it's just the same,
We could not last a single flame;
His glory far too much to take,
Our frailty would wholly break;
To look directly at His face
Would see us gone, without a trace.

These bodies we inhabit now,
To have it all, will not allow;
So, still far off, we have to stay,
For our advantage, kept at bay.

Yet on the road that Jesus trod,
We can see so much more of God;
For by His being on the Earth,
We have a sense of all He's worth;
Although, for now, our view is dim,
We see the Father's heart through Him.

To look to Jesus every day
Will lead us to a different way;
For this is how God draws us near,
His Spirit speaking truth so clear;
We're safely distanced, yet close by:
Though still far off, He lifts us high.

In Plain Sight

If only we had seen how much was hidden in plain sight,
If we'd known then what we know now, then, perhaps, we might
Have viewed things in a different way, to take another tack;
Determined to look forward, instead of looking back.

If we had seen the rocks before we were so wholly wrecked,
If we had tried to steer away, not stumbling on unchecked;
Then, perhaps, we might have seen we'd backed a losing horse,
And how we might be winners, if we let You set the course.

If we had seen the wood, not just the trees, in endless rows,
And understood the ways in which your grace and mercy flows,
Then, perhaps, it's possible it would have saved us grief,
If we had looked to your sure hand, in bringing us relief.

If we'd not left our heads too often buried in the sand,
Till we're becoming strangers in the strangest kind of land;
Then, perhaps, we may have shifted focus to a view
That, if we'd kept on going, would have led us straight to You.

If we had kept our eyes upon the only One to trust,
Instead of clinging on to worthless things condemned to rust,
Then, perhaps, our hearts might have been taken to a place,
Freed to kneel in awe and praise, to truly seek your face.

If only we could see how much is hidden in plain sight:
The way to our salvation clearly standing in the light,
Then, perhaps, from You we would no longer be estranged,
And all would turn their face to You, and be forever changed!

SONGS OF LOVING

God is love. Whoever lives in love lives in God, and God in him. In this way, love is made complete among us so that we will have confidence on the day of judgment, because in this world we are like him. There is no fear in love. But perfect love drives out fear...

1 John 4:16-18

To love and be loved

Love is at the heart of everything God is and God does. Not romantic or brotherly love, but what in the Greek is referred to as 'agape' love: sacrificial, selfless and self-giving, where meeting the needs of others and ensuring their wellbeing becomes the focus and purpose of our lives.

It is beyond our frail mortal capacity to love as unconditionally or as deeply as God loves us. All we are able to do is aspire to emulate his example as best we can, striving to love others in our own imperfect way; and, in doing so, sharing at least glimpses of the Father's love with those who might otherwise never encounter him.

This kind of love is a real game-changer; when we come to appreciate the depth of God's love for us individually, nothing can ever be the same again.

God loves us as we are, no strings attached: but how often do we struggle to accept that for ourselves?

Unlike our fickle human nature, God is constant and unchanging and he can be trusted absolutely. It is so much easier to love ourselves when we are graced with the certainty that there is someone who accepts us just as we are and who will, no matter what, love us unconditionally.

Love Beyond

What am I to make of God's grace, beyond measure?
His care everlasting eclipses my love;
Freely given and yet the most precious of treasure,
Surpassing my hope, standing shoulders above.

The love that He shares is beyond understanding,
The depths that it reaches go deeper than deep;
Yet it's finding its way to a perfect soft landing,
The slope He will climb for me, never too steep.

Even if all my love can't come close to His giving,
In my imperfect way, I can give it my best,
Seeking out something better, a new type of living,
With all of myself, and let God do the rest.

Although there's not much I can bring to the table,
And it's hard enough just to find love for my own,
Still, I do what I can, with the little I'm able:
It is only by planting, a seed may be grown.

Standing in awe of this grace, such a blessing,
My trust in my own worth is cut down to size;
Loved as I am, He does not need impressing:
Matchless, His love is my undeserved prize.

To give me the Kingdom, the Father's good pleasure,
Through love that's transforming, a paradigm shift;
I can but give praise for this glorious treasure,
And marvel once more at His wonderful gift.

Country

If love becomes the country where we live,
We'll find we all have so much more to give;
If selflessness the only badge we wear,
We'll find it so much easier to share.

If we know giving as the real gift,
The clouds will part, we'll see the darkness lift;
Instead of looking out for number one,
We'll find there is a better race to run.

By setting to one side our empty need,
The shackles of indifference are freed.
In place of grasping all we think we're owed,
Let's choose the reconciliation road.

If we seek out the lost, as yet unknown,
The seeds of restoration can be sown.
For if we see them with the Father's eyes,
He'll lead us to a place to still their cries.

And so, whatever faith, belief, or creed,
All people have this fundamental need
For being prized; by prizing others too,
We'll see a new perspective seeping through.

God made us for each other, not alone,
It's time to set a unifying tone.
In the Creator's image we are made:
And when we shine, we'll see His love displayed.

No Small Thing

It's no small thing to be loved by God,
To know He'll always hold us tight;
As one, like two peas in a pod:
We flourish in His soothing light.

It isn't ours to take as read,
We cannot earn our special place;
Instead, we trust in all He said:
It's no small thing, His gift of grace.

It's no small thing to have a friend
Who will not ever let us down;
He leads us to the perfect end:
He clothes us in the whitest gown.

It isn't ours to win the prize
By anything we might have done;
Our prideful selves cut down to size:
It's no small thing, to know God's Son.

It's no small thing to count the cost,
For us He gave His every breath;
Just when it seemed that all was lost,
Our Lord forever conquered death.

To know He's always on our side
Should make our hearts rejoice and sing;
It's no small thing, and undenied:
To be loved by God is the greatest thing!

One Size Fits All

There's no favourite with God, there's no discrimination,
He longs to transform us, restoring Creation;
It's all buttoned up, from the short to the tall:
When it comes to His love, it's one size fits us all.

There is no one too bad, He wants none to be lost,
For it was for us all that He paid such a cost;
There is no one too poor, it is ours to afford,
If we put aside self and accept Him as Lord;
We don't need any coin, there's no payment to call,
For the grace that is offered is one size fits all.

There is no advantage that we can accrue,
Despite all the good that we think we might do,
We cannot earn His favour, it's offered for free,
It's His power alone makes the dark from us flee;
It's all tailored for us, with His eye on the ball:
Sin's measure is taken, one size fits us all.

No longer patched up and worn out at the knee,
It's the fabric of all that He made us to be
That is ours, in the finest array to be suited,
The trends of the past into touch firmly booted,
Forgotten, forever, no need to recall:
When it comes to His love, it's one size fits us all.

Unchanging

Though my resolve is fickle and so frail,
A steadfastness that struggles to prevail,
With your unending love set at the core,
Your Word is always certain, ever sure.

Though I descend into the deepest slumber,
My countless chances, missing, without number,
You have for me a fully worked equation,
That leads me to a perfect combination.

Though I may change my mind like changing clothing,
You stand by your commitment, like betrothing,
A promise that your love is set forever,
That none of my evasiveness can sever.

Though I can't see which way the wind is blowing,
Too quick to fool myself that I'm all-knowing,
You yet would see me follow a new trending,
To save me from a cruel and bitter ending.

Though all of my consistency's fast leaking,
That leaves me, in the moment, ever seeking,
Your story is writ large upon the pages,
That stands, unchanged, forever through the ages.

Although I fail to follow your direction,
You're always holding me in true affection;
You are the same, as from the first beginning,
My hapless soul determined to be winning.

Though I too often change my heart and mind,
And leave the better part of me behind,
You never change; your heart is set on mine:
Yours is the light that never fails to shine.

Love Always (a song)

A reflection on 1 Corinthians 13:7-8

When darkest thoughts my life reflects:
- Love fills the breach, my soul protects;
When all the World holds precious, rusts:
- Love never fails, love always trusts;
When faith is tested, on the ropes:
- Love never fails, love always hopes;
And in the face of all my fears:
- Love never fails, love perseveres.

Chorus
Love never fades, love never fails,
Love shines the light that never pales;
Love sets the course and fills the sails,
Love never fades, God's love prevails.

When safety's gone, protection fled,
- Love wraps me in its arms, instead.
When trust seems distant, out of reach,
- Love comes again, to fill the breach.
When all seems lost, when hope recedes,
- Love's gently there, to meet my needs.
My perseverance, hard to find:
- Love calms my soul and soothes my mind.

Chorus

Although the World might say that love is going out of fashion,
Your love is never far away, to sweep me off my feet;
You fill my longing heart with faith, with hope and with compassion,
Your love restores my soul again, to make my life complete:

Chorus

Songs of Passion

Do not merely listen to the word, and so deceive yourselves.
Do what it says.

James 1:22

For the kingdom of God is not a matter of talk but of power.

1 Corinthians 4:20

...let us not love with words or tongue but with actions and
in truth.

1 John 3:18

Giving our all

The Christian life is not one of passivity, sitting in a quiet corner, waiting patiently for Heaven to arrive. The Kingdom of Heaven is about God's love stirring us to action and about our bringing his truth into the light.

God has gone to extraordinary lengths for us: he has replaced our tears of weeping with tears of joy; he has liberated us from the power of sin and death; he has secured our eternal salvation; and he has restored us to an unbreakable and intimate relationship with him as our eternal Father.

There is no place for half measures; he fills our cup to overflowing and we should similarly be pouring out all our energies in our praise and honour of him and in ensuring that we share the wonderful good news of Jesus with the rest of the World.

When we truly appreciate the enormity of all he has done for us, how can we be anything less than set alight with passion for him?

New Fire

If God's call on our lives we will truly be heeding,
Then new fire is what we most surely are needing;
To reignite fervour, we have to be bolder,
And not be content just to let kindling smoulder.

From lives of indifference completely estranged,
We have to push forward, commit to be changed;
If we're truly to follow in more than just name
We must let His love burn, reach within for the flame.

He fuels us for action, refined in the fire,
We must turn up the heat, raise the temperature higher;
We must hear Jesus' calling, with hearts that are stilled,
By His Spirit, each day, being constantly filled.

If it isn't of God and it's just about man,
Then every scheme, every grandiose plan
Is so little of worth and consigned to the trash,
To be thrown in the hearth and reduced to mere ash.

We must unleash the heart that within us is stored,
From a spark to a blaze that cannot be ignored;
We must shine new horizons at dawn every day,
For His light must be seen and not hidden away.

Stoking His fire should be all our yearning,
With flames ever higher and constantly burning;
When we declare truth, with a passion that's real,
It is then He enables our sealing the deal.

Pilot Light

It isn't enough if it's only glowing,
Burning so dimly, our eagerness slowing;
The danger is real when the ardour is fading:
It's like we're in quicksand, with steps heavy wading.

The flame flickers lower, we need reignition
If we're to deliver our God-given mission;
We must not put it out: when the Spirit is burning
Deep in our hearts, He will meet every yearning.

To turn up the pilot light, we need a new fire,
The Spirit to move, for our faith to fly higher;
Only He has the means for transforming our days:
With His hand on our lives, He can set us ablaze.

New Clothes

Too long the same old clothes we've worn:
Though frayed and tattered, faded, torn,
Our comfort in the things we know,
It's hard to think of letting go.

Buttoned up and standing still,
We find it hard to seek God's will;
Instead of making do and mend,
He calls us to a different trend.

For with our cover wearing thin,
The need for change is pressing in;
His Spirit works in changing fashion:
Ignites in us transforming passion.

Much more than just another patch,
We need to find a different match;
His Spirit's call is pushing through,
For us to put on something new.

Baptised in Him, so fully blessed,
In Jesus we are newly dressed
In clothing that cannot be priced:
Invaluable, the love of Christ!

Excite

If Jesus truly is our Lord,
He should be worshipped and adored
In all we do, with every word,
Our heart and soul so deeply stirred;
Assured that victory has been won,
That we are loved by God's own Son,
A love that sparks a new beginning,
Forever breaks the hold of sinning;
The strongholds of the darkness stormed,
Releasing us for life transformed,
Down alleys blind no longer driven,
Though we were lost, we're now forgiven,
And by His grace forever freed,
To let Him meet our every need.

The emptiness that once we chased
By trust in Him should be replaced,
To lead us on an upward slope,
To greater heights of love and hope;
A faith that surely should ignite
So many reasons to excite
The very fibre of our being,
From every unmet longing freeing.

With all to venture, much to gain,
This is a joy we can't contain,
A love we simply have to share,
To flood the World with Heaven's care;
To spend our every waking hour
As if we stand in lofty tower,
With voices that forever raise
Our songs of never-ending praise!

SONGS OF PRAYER

The Lord is near. Do not be anxious about anything, but in everything, by prayer and petition, with thanksgiving, present your requests to God. And the peace of God, which transcends all understanding, will guard your hearts and your minds in Christ Jesus.

Philippians 4: 5-7

Loud and clear

In any healthy personal relationship, communication is vital.

God communicates with us in many different ways: to name but a few, through our reading the Bible, through our experience in worship (most commonly in song), through our interaction with other people (their words and actions) and through the general circumstances of our lives.

All these are important, but one that is particularly key is prayer. A regular, committed, and meaningful dialogue with our Heavenly Father is critical to growing our relationship with him. But prayer should not just be seen as our presenting a 'shopping list' to God, waiting passively for him to fill our baskets with what we think will fulfil us.

Prayer is a two-way street. Bringing our wants and needs, our hopes, our struggles and our pleas for help to God are right and proper things to do. But we also need actively and daily to be listening to God, both as he responds to our particular requests, but more generally as he speaks his purposes and direction into our lives.

Every prayer is heard; and every prayer is answered – but not necessarily with the answer that we were expecting or hoping for. Too often, blinded by the moment, we think we know the best way forward for our lives; but God always knows better. He protects us from (what are for us unforeseen) consequences of things we ask for that would ultimately harm us, sometimes asking us to wait until the time is right, and at other times completely closing the door, in order to save us from ourselves.

But his every response to our prayers is made as a loving and caring Father, who only wants to give us his good things for our lives. We may not see it now, but we will understand later on the many ways in which we are constantly blessed by God's guiding hand upon our lives. We may set ourselves up to fail, but if we trust and follow him, God makes us winners in the end.

So, we need to develop patience, and understanding that (unlike ours) God's purposes for our lives are always for our benefit and that his timing is perfect. We may not get the answer we were hoping for, or we may have to wait for the answer for far longer than we would like. But God will deliver.

God is speaking to us all the time, but we too often walk around with our fingers in our ears and miss so much that would serve us well, if only we allowed ourselves ears to hear.

Cultivating a habit of setting aside quality time for waiting on God in prayer can reap amazing spiritual – and practical – rewards.

Sooner

If we removed the fingers from our ears,
We'd lose so many dark, unfounded fears;
We'd know the reassurance of His care,
A love that He is reaching out to share:
We'd know His voice, and wish we'd done it sooner.

If we removed the fingers from our ears,
And let Him share our hurting and our tears,
He'd guide us, so much surer, on the road,
He'd take the strain and bear our heavy load:
We'd stand and look towards His coming sooner.

If we could clear distractions from our eyes,
We'd see Creation etched across the skies.
His Lordship shown in everything that's made,
We'd know His power and never be afraid:
We'd sense His touch and wish we'd done it sooner.

If we could see right through familiar lies,
A World that pulls the wool over our eyes –
Too often, precious moments lost, betrayed,
The times we know we could – and should – have prayed:
With open hearts, we would have seen Him sooner.

If just for once, we'd put aside the day,
And let Him, through His Spirit, have His way;
If we removed the fingers from our ears,
We'd hear Him now – not just when He appears:
And wonder why we didn't do it sooner.

Pray

There's a sense of expectancy, ours to create,
Not a prayer is unanswered and none go unheard,
God hears every request, values every word,
But His timing is sovereign, we may have to wait.

It ebbs and it flows into real conversations,
Relieving our doubts and assuaging our fear;
To speak and to listen, be open to hear,
We draw close to our Father and build true relations.

Our cries for His mercy are never rejected,
Assured of His love, He will answer our call;
He will help us to climb the unscalable wall,
Although sometimes in ways we could not have expected.

It's ours to embrace every day, hour by hour,
If we seek out His heart, with our pride deeply swallowed,
If we pray in the Spirit, His will to be followed:
Then we'll truly experience prayer's awesome power.

Breathe

We cannot choose to breathe, but we can seek a different air;
When we are ready in our heart to turn our ear to prayer,
Then we might hear that still small voice that whispers something new,
And we might feel the wind of change come blowing gently through.

We cannot choose to breathe, but we can seek a different space;
When we are ready in our heart for other dreams to chase;
And when we pray, that still small voice may call us to take rest,
To put aside the striving that can leave us so hard pressed.

We cannot choose to breathe, but we can seek a different aim;
When we are ready in our heart for more than just the same,
Approaching He who gives us life, with openness to pray:
That still small voice that calls to us is just a breath away.

Two-Way Street

Prayer's a gift God's planted
That we should not take for granted:
It's not something we have earned;
The depth of Jesus' caring
Makes us bolder in our sharing,
Though there's still much to be learned.

Prayer can be surprising,
When we see new targets rising,
Hitting home, the aim is true;
If we're open, really hearing,
There's no reason to be fearing
Arrows landing somewhere new.

Prayer is freely flowing
In the confidence of knowing
That He longs to draw us near;
When His company we're seeking,
We will hear Him softly speaking
With a truth that's ringing clear.

Prayer is ours for choosing,
It's for winning, not for losing,
But we have to be prepared
To make a real connection,
To be open to direction
By the truths that may be shared.

Prayer's for daily living,
There's so much He will be giving
When we let our soul be stirred;
Ever in His love abiding,
He will lead us, surely guiding
By the wonder of His Word.

Prayer's not just us talking,
It's a two-way street we're walking,
When we make the better choice;
In true anticipation
Of a deeper conversation,
As we come to know His voice.

Speaking

Whatever else we hope for, or are seeking,
Above it all, we need to hear God speaking,
Delivering salvation through forgiving:
The Word of God the way to holy living.

For looking to ourselves cannot avail us,
With turning ever inward sure to fail us;
But when our needs in prayer we bring, confessing,
We will receive the greatest of all blessing.

Determined perseverance in our praying
Will see our every fear the Lord allaying;
When we receive the wisdom He's imparting,
It's then real transformation can be starting.

It's not about the way we may be feeling;
In making time to come before Him, kneeling,
Instead, is something that is ours for choosing:
He answers every prayer, never refusing.

The barriers won't fall unless we shake them,
And prayer has all the power we need to break them;
And once the walls are down, the silence broken,
God's power is felt in every word that's spoken.

Whatever else we search for, or are hoping,
In our own strength, it's not enough for coping;
But when the Saviour's voice our hearts are seeking,
By truly listening, we will hear Him speaking.

Songs of Sharing

Then Jesus came to them and said, "All authority in heaven and on earth has been given to me. Therefore go and make disciples of all nations, baptising them in the name of the Father and of the Son and of the Holy Spirit, and teaching them to obey everything I have commanded you..."

Matthew 28:18-20

Telling others

Our principal calling as Christians is to share the good news of Jesus with others.

So how are we doing? Why does the message so often seem to fall on deaf ears? Perhaps sometimes we don't try hard enough (or at all); but at other times, maybe we try too much...?

What we too often fail to remember is that it is not about what we do, but about God: only the power of his Holy Spirit acting in people's lives can change hearts.

Without him, all our efforts, however well-intentioned, will come to nothing. It's only when we truly partner with him, and trust him to use us as he wills, that we can really make a difference.

We have our part to play: in bringing God's love to others, we have to be truly ready and willing to be his hands and feet; but to do things his way.

383

Hero to Zero

When others are hurt, at the end of their rope,
We should always be ready to offer them hope;
When they feel that their light's snatched away like a thief,
We must shine out a love that will bring them relief.

Though it may seem for nothing, once they are relieved,
All too quick to forget all the prayers they received;
But, remember, God works in a heart that is seeking,
If just for a moment they hear Jesus speaking,
A seed may be planted, the Spirit can grow it,
For they may have been changed even when they don't know it.

Two millennia gone and yet time moves so fast
That there seems little distance from now to the past;
Back then, from His lips, every stronghold was broken,
Still today, by the Spirit, the same Word is spoken.
And when Jesus spoke, something new all were hearing,
His words had such power, they sensed Heaven nearing,
Convinced this was something unique that they heard,
They all found themselves hanging on every word.

For just a short time, all their voices were raised,
Here was surely a man who deserved to be praised;
And yet, just as quickly, their hearts had been turned,
When His words cut so deep and their consciences burned;
Too hard to be looking themselves in the face,
Content to retreat to their previous place.

One moment, a man who was highly respected,
The next, one reviled and completely rejected;
How can a person, with such good to say,
Go from hero to zero in less than a day?
If we carry His Cross, we'll expect nothing less:
Yet, in ways we can't see, we still comfort and bless;
All our hope should be set on no other reward
Than humbly to serve in the name of the Lord.

Filling Our Nets

When God has joined us in the boat,
He more than keeps our souls afloat;
What serving others often gets
Are teeming fish and bursting nets.

If by His hand our nets are cast,
To put Him first instead of last,
He'll guide us surely to a place
Of mercy, love and boundless grace.

Nets empty when alone we tried,
He bids us look the other side:
Where, with His help, we may begin
To rein His great provision in.

Though such abundance in the catch,
The surface this can barely scratch
Of all the bounty that He brings:
The promise of eternal things.

He leads us safely back to shore,
Then out again, delivers more,
No longer on an even keel,
Unlimited, the catch to reel.

When we have reached our final port,
He'll look with joy on all we've caught:
It's our response to Jesus' call
That lands this great, eternal haul.

If by His hand our sails are set,
There is no fear in getting wet;
For when we put our Saviour first,
We should expect our nets to burst!

Bring Revival

We cry 'Lord, bring revival!' and yet we find survival
Is the best that we can do;
But if we want revival to make a sure arrival,
We must look to something new.

To truly seek His leading, acknowledging our needing
Of His amazing love,
Will find our fear receding, when we're hungry to be feeding
On His power from above.

We hear the distant drumming of revival that is coming
To a hurting, broken land;
Instead of holding steady, we must each be ever ready
To be counted, make a stand.

The Holy Spirit frees us to spread the word of Jesus,
Freely give to all we meet;
But we must be ever willing, in our holy task fulfilling:
For we are His hands and feet.

We cannot keep ignoring the souls set for restoring,
As He's longing to break through;
The truth is not for fighting, revival needs igniting:
And it starts with me and you.

Save

I want to save this city, every person living in it;
If this is some strange contest, then I really want to win it;
I want to see Christ on the stage, the victory rostrum manning,
To be the sure result of this great strategy He's planning.

I want to save my family, and others I'm befriending,
Who haven't come to know Him yet, before they reach an ending;
I long to see such change afoot, with hearts thrown open wide,
I want to help all those I love meet on the other side;
I want to see His precious Book each hopeful heart fulfilling,
Those words that speak a deeper truth, to change us if we're willing;
So they'll embrace the One alone who's making all things right,
To learn just what it means to live by faith, and not by sight.

I want to see God's Kingdom breaking through in greater measure,
The force of all the Spirit's power no longer buried treasure;
The fullness of God's grace for which Creation has been waiting,
His justice and His mercy every soul illuminating.

I want to see the World renewed, the sting of death denying,
But this is not a purchase that I have the means of buying;
It's only Jesus' perfect love that has the power to do it,
It's He who makes the sacrifice, and me who puts Him through it.

I cannot be the one who's left, still standing at the station;
I have to keep on moving, closer to our destination;
I need to take the road that leads me onwards, ever higher,
To places He's already made, to be my whole desire.

I long to save this city, but it's not of my own doing;
It has to be the movement of His Spirit I'm pursuing;
By taking this small step of faith, to make a small beginning,
Means nothing is impossible and all is His for winning.

Songs of the Spirit

[Jesus said] "When the Counsellor comes, whom I will send to you from the Father, the Spirit of truth who goes out from the Father, he will testify about me."

John 15:26

Come, Holy Spirit

Historically, the Holy Spirit has had some bad press: the traditional description of a 'holy ghost' has unfortunately tended to conjure up a sense of the unnatural, accompanied by fearful images of the disembodied dead, whose only purpose is to haunt and terrify.

But nothing could be further from the truth.

The Holy Spirit is a real – albeit supernatural – person; the third aspect of the three in one God, alongside the Father and the Son. His function is not to scare us, but to help us, to guide us, to comfort us and most particularly to give us 24/7 access to and intimate connectivity with God the Father.

As Christians, we have the continual presence of God's love living within us through his Spirit. But, like an engine that needs to be refuelled, we must be continually coming back to God, seeking an ever-greater infilling of his Spirit. In doing so, we will ensure that our tank will not run dry and that we will be equipped to pour out God's love to those around us

Hear

The Spirit dwells within you,
But He isn't as you are;
Though to the World invisible,
He's brighter than a star.

Though He is not for holding,
You may not take His hand,
The tangible intangible
Is just as God has planned.

You do not see Him standing,
At least, not with your eyes,
Yet you can recognise Him,
He carries no disguise.

Your arms cannot enfold Him,
Though He is touching you;
You do not meet Him face to face,
Yet know what He can do.

You do not hear Him speaking,
At least, not in your ears;
Yet sense His firm assurance
As He deals with all your fears.

You don't share conversation,
Not His, the spoken word;
Yet what He has to say to you
Is deep within you stirred.

You don't see His arriving
When He is passing through;
But once He's been invited,
He is making all things new.

When you are seeking comfort,
His arms are open wide;
And when you ask for counsel,
Then His Word will be your guide.

He loves you like a father,
He's more than just a friend,
And you can be yourself with Him,
You never need pretend.

He isn't of this World, like you,
Yet still completely real;
He meets your daily hunger
And provides your every meal.

When the Spirit dwells within you,
He adopts you as His own;
In making you His dwelling place,
You'll never be alone.

Overflowing

When we look to ourselves and forget the Lord's leading,
Although striving so much, we will not be succeeding;
All the sweetness we search for too soon will turn sour,
As we struggle to move in our own fragile power.

With our cup full of holes, we can't stop it from leaking,
We must look for His filling, to hear the Lord speaking;
When our levels are low, there's great comfort in knowing
As we drink from His well, we will be overflowing
With goodness and grace that He gives us for sharing;
Though our cloak may be threadbare, He makes it hardwearing,
Equipped for the task, seeking God, never doubt Him,
With certainty nothing's completed without Him.

So, let's show ourselves least, give the Lord every glory,
For it's all about Him, it's not ours, it's His story;
Secure in His love, and not letting fear seize us,
To know all we need has been given in Jesus;
There's no adding or taking away, there is just Him:
We'll be filled to the full, and beyond, when we trust Him.

Refill

In and yet not of this World,
Although God's sons and daughters,
Our souls, laid bare to everything,
Are caught in darker waters.

When mixes wash away from God,
Allegiances disputed,
The subtle drift down other streams
Sees our resolve diluted.

Overfilled with worldly cares,
The seams that hold us creaking,
How often do we fail to see,
So much of Him is leaking?

Distractions, pouring in like waves
Can puncture and assail us;
Without the Spirit's constant flow,
Our strength will surely fail us.

It isn't just a one-time call,
This gift we should be prizing;
We need to seek His power anew,
Each day, re-energising.

A love that forms the perfect mix,
To calm our souls and still us;
When we invite God's Spirit in,
He'll never fail to fill us.

The Making of Me (a song)

Why do I run and never pause to hear your soothing voice?
Though you're the One, too often I pursue another choice;
Because of grace, I've nothing left to prove:
I should be counting every blessing,
Instead of second-guessing
Your next move…

Chorus 1

So take me, and shake me,
Let your Spirit overtake me,
To recapture what went missing at the tree.
So take me, and shake me,
For I know You won't forsake me:
You will always be the making of me.

Why do I hide? Your longing is to bring me home, once more;
You put aside your glory, your Creation to restore;
Because of love, You saved me from the start,
I should be giving You my needing,
And in faith embrace the leading
of my heart…

Chorus 2

So take me, and break me,
Let your Spirit come, reshape me,
Renew my soul to set my living free.
So take me, and break me
For I know You won't forsake me:
You will always be the making of me.

Why should I fear, with open arms You wait for me:
Chains disappear, my sin erased, You set me free;
Because of hope, my spirit comes to rest,
I should just fall, amazed, before You,
And in humility adore You,
Fully blessed…

Chorus 3

So take me, remake me,
Let your Spirit rise to wake me,
Revive my soul to all that it should be.
So take me, remake me,
For I know You won't forsake me:
You will always be the making of me.

So take me, and break me,
Reshape and re-awake me…
For You will always be the making of me.

SONGS OF WISDOM

"The fear of the Lord is the beginning of wisdom, and knowledge of the Holy One is understanding."

Proverbs 9:10

Who is wise and understanding among you? Let him show it by his good life, by deeds done in the humility that comes from wisdom…the wisdom that comes from heaven is first of all pure; then peace-loving, considerate, submissive, full of mercy and good fruit, impartial and sincere.

James 3:13, 17

A wiser God

In the currency of the World, great value is often attached to the sort of wisdom that someone has garnered from a lifetime's experiences. While by no means universally the case, there are many instances where elderly people show themselves to be particularly worldly-wise, when blessed with a perspective that only a long life well spent can provide.

But there is only so much that one person can ever learn or know; and that is still only a drop in the ocean, when compared to the omniscient nature of God.

From a Christian perspective, whatever our age or stage in life, true wisdom comes not from life's experiences, but from an awe and appreciation of who God is and what he has done for us.

This is not generated from within ourselves, but rather is produced by the Holy Spirit working in our lives.

The truly wise person understands their own personal limitations and will confidently look for guidance and direction for their life from 'the only wise God' (Romans 16:27).

Wisdom Remembered

Forget all the baubles you're sold,
God's wisdom is worth more than gold;
His Spirit at work, making whole,
Seeding value in every soul.

Forget what you once counted most,
Don't be fooled by the World's empty boast;
The vain calling to put ourselves first
Is a bubble too soon to be burst.

Forget all the things you have done,
Looking out only for number one;
When you put selfish need to one side,
His peace in your heart will abide.

Forget what you thought you had learned,
That anything good must be earned;
If you open your heart, you will see
That God's love and forgiveness are free.

Forget what you've often been told,
That it's too late to change now you're old;
Transformation is always at hand,
To deliver His purpose, as planned.

So, remember, His promise is true,
Self-sufficiency fading from view
Is the way that His blessings will flow,
As He leads you the way you should go.
And never forget to recall,
Though deserving of nothing at all,
By His grace we will fully receive:
All He asks us to do is believe.

Lacking

It's said that wisdom comes with age, but I began to wonder
If this is just another false impression that I'm under;
For when I look back all those years, I don't seem any smarter
Than when I'd only just begun, naive, a hopeful starter.

Imagining I have the strength for every dam unblocking,
Or that I hold the keys I need for every door unlocking,
Or when I think I've solved the clues, the case now set for cracking:
I find out how far short I fall, how much I'm really lacking.

Yet caught by these assumptions under which I wrongly labour,
Too ready to believe my powers far exceed my neighbour,
Presuming insight's mine from just the passing of the years,
This empty, vain, illusion carves a path to many tears.

I only have to look, it's ever there before my eyes:
Without my Saviour's leading, I am really not that wise.

Though there are things of use I may have learned along the way,
Too often, still, I find it hard to know the words to say;
When looking only to myself, too eager to persist,
I realise my limits, the wise counsel that I missed.

When there are only roadblocks, too familiar, left to meet,
With all my old behaviours stuck forever on repeat:
I need to turn my face to Him, to open up my eyes,
Surrendering my will, to let humility arise.

The truth will sadly out, it could be sooner, may be later;
Without control, I'm all at sea, it's like I'm on a freighter
That doesn't have a pilot, runaway and wildly veering
Towards the rocks; abandoned, with nobody fit for steering.

Though I may fool myself that I'm completely in control,
There's so much I am lacking, that it leaves a gaping hole;
Without His grace and wisdom, I am sinking ever deeper,
The little I can bring is losing value, growing cheaper.

With so much left to learn, then, it should come as no surprise,
To realise the truth that I am really not that wise.

Real wisdom is the awe of knowing God is in control,
That He provides the way to truth for each surrendered soul;
Accepting just how small I am, to wait for Him to guide:
Equipping me with all that only Jesus can provide.

Not Knowing

If I knew how everything was going to turn out,
Saw it all with certainty and never left in doubt;
If I knew the story's end before I read the book,
So sure of everything unseen, without a second look;
If I knew a future that was written from the start,
Familiar with every word and knew it off by heart,
If I'd read the storyline ahead of chapter one,
Discovering each plotted twist before I had begun;
If I knew the ups and downs and how each would occur,
The hope of what the future holds would have no need to stir;
I'd sing the final note before the first beat of the drum,
I'd know the very best and worst of everything to come.

Without the opportunity of changing or amending,
I'd have to sit and watch the film run to its certain ending,
I wouldn't need to trust in God for what tomorrow holds,
Or let Him be my guiding light as every day unfolds;
I'd miss out on the wonder of the intimacy of prayer,
Of all those precious moments that we otherwise might share;
There'd be no great adventure, nor the chance to be new grown,
Nor find new paths that otherwise I never could have known;
I wouldn't have the treasured gift of drinking in His Word,
To let the longing in my soul by Him be daily stirred;
With everything already known, I'd only look to me:
But this is not a circumstance to ever set me free.

The strangeness of not knowing should be cherished in my heart,
Content, this side of Heaven, I will only see in part;
Assured the good that waits for me will have the final say,
That all will be as it should be, when Jesus leads the way;
It's when I reach a perfect end that all will be revealed,
For my eternal resting place in Him is surely sealed!

RE - #0009 - 280824 - C54 - 234/172/24 - PB - 9781914002489 - Gloss Lamination